POINTS OF VIEW

POINTS OF VIEW

by
T. S. ELIOT

FABER AND FABER LTD
24 Russell Square
London

*First published in June Mcmxli
by Faber and Faber Limited
24 Russell Square London W.C.1
Printed in Great Britain by
Western Printing Services Ltd. Bristol*

NOTE

~~~~~

This selection of T. S. Eliot's critical writings has been made and edited, with the author's approval, by John Hayward. It contains representative passages, ranging from a single paragraph to a complete essay, and has been designed as an introduction to the author's work in prose. Titles have been supplied by the editor and the source and date of composition are given at the end of each passage.

SELECT BIBLIOGRAPHY
of Prose Writings

Thomas Stearns Eliot, born 1888. *Selected Essays,*
1932. The Use of Poetry and the Use of Criticism,
1933. After Strange Gods, 1934. Elizabethan Essays,
1934. Essays Ancient and Modern, 1936. The Idea of
a Christian Society, 1939.

CONTENTS

~~~~~

Part I—Literary Criticism

Part II—Dramatic Criticism

7

Contents

Part III—Individual Authors

Part IV—Religion and Society

Part 1

LITERARY CRITICISM

THE FUNCTION OF CRITICISM

From time to time, every hundred years or so, it is desirable that some critic shall appear to review the past of our literature, and set the poets and the poems in a new order. This task is not one of revolution but of readjustment. What we observe is partly the same scene, but in a different and more distant perspective; there are new and strange objects in the foreground, to be drawn accurately in proportion to the more familiar ones which now approach the horizon, where all but the most eminent become invisible to the naked eye. The exhaustive critic, armed with a powerful glass, will be able to sweep the distance and gain an acquaintance with minute objects in the landscape with which to compare minute objects close at hand; he will be able to gauge nicely the position and proportion of the objects surrounding us, in the whole of the vast panorama. This metaphorical fancy only represents the ideal; but Dryden, Johnson, and Arnold have each performed the task as well as human frailty will allow. The majority of critics can be expected only to parrot the opinions of the last master of criticism; among more independent minds a period of destruction, of pre-

posterous over-estimation, and of successive fash-
ions takes place, until a new authority comes to in-
troduce some order. And it is not merely the passage of time and accumulation of new artistic experience, nor the ineradicable tendency of the great
majority of men to repeat the opinions of those few
who have taken the trouble to think, nor the tendency of a nimble but myopic minority to progene-
rate heterodoxies, that makes new assessments necessary. It is that no generation is interested in Art in
quite the same way as any other; each generation,
like each individual, brings to the contemplation of
art its own categories of appreciation, makes its own
demands upon art, and has its own uses for art.
"Pure" artistic appreciation is to my thinking only
an ideal, when not merely a figment, and must be, so
long as the appreciation of art is an affair of limited
and transient human beings existing in space and
time. Both artist and audience are limited. There is
for each time, for each artist, a kind of alloy required
to make the metal workable into art; and each generation prefers its own alloy to any other. Hence each
new master of criticism performs a useful service
merely by the fact that his errors are of a different
kind from the last; and the longer the sequence of
critics we have, the greater amount of correction is
possible.

[From *The Use of Poetry and the Use of Criticism*:
Matthew Arnold. 1933.]

CRITICISM

Criticism must always profess an end in view, which roughly speaking, appears to be the elucidation of works of art and the correction of taste. The critic's task, therefore, appears to be quite clearly cut out for him; and it ought to be comparatively easy to decide whether he performs it satisfactorily, and in general, what kinds of criticism are useful and what are otiose. But on giving the matter a little attention, we perceive that criticism, far from being a simple and orderly field of beneficent activity, from which impostors can be readily ejected, is no better than a Sunday park of contending and contentious orators, who have not even arrived at the articulation of their differences. Here, one would suppose, was a place for quiet co-operative labour. The critic, one would suppose, if he is to justify his existence, should endeavour to discipline his personal prejudices and cranks—tares to which we are all subject —and compose his differences with as many of his fellows as possible, in the common pursuit of true judgement. When we find that quite the contrary prevails, we begin to suspect that the critic owes his livelihood to the violence and extremity of his opposition to other critics, or else to some trifling oddities of his own with which he contrives to season the opinions which men already hold, and which out of vanity or sloth they prefer to maintain. We are tempted to expel the lot.

Immediately after such an eviction, or as soon as relief has abated our rage, we are compelled to admit that there remain certain books, certain essays, certain sentences, certain men, who have been "useful" to us. And our next step is to attempt to classify these, and find out whether we establish any principles for deciding what kinds of book should be preserved, and what aims and methods of criticism should be followed.

We must ourselves decide what is useful to us and what is not; and it is quite likely that we are not competent to decide. But it is fairly certain that "interpretation" (I am not touching upon the acrostic element in literature) is only legitimate when it is not interpretation at all, but merely putting the reader in possession of facts which he would otherwise have missed. I have had some experience of Extension lecturing, and I have found only two ways of leading any pupils to like anything with the right liking: to present them with a selection of the simple kind of facts about a work—its conditions, its setting, its genesis—or else to spring the work on them in such a way that they were not prepared to be prejudiced against it.

Comparison and analysis are the chief tools of the critic. It is obvious indeed that they *are* tools, to be handled with care, and not employed in an inquiry into the number of times giraffes are mentioned in the English novel. They are not used with conspicuous success by many contemporary writers. You must know what to compare and what to analyse. The late Professor Ker had skill in the use of these tools. Comparison and analysis need only the cadavers on the table; but interpretation is always producing parts of the body from its pockets, and fixing them in place. And any book, any essay, any note in *Notes and Queries*, which produces a fact even of the lowest order about a work of art is a better piece of work than nine-tenths of the most pretentious critical journalism, in journals or in books. We assume, of course, that we are masters and not servants of facts, and that we know that the discovery of Shakespeare's laundry bills would not be of much use to us; but we must always reserve final judgement as to the futility of the research which has discovered them, in the possibility that some genius will appear who will know of a use to which to put them. Scholarship, even in its humblest forms, has its rights; we assume that we know how to use it, and how to neglect it. Of course the multiplication of critical books and essays may create, and I have seen it create, a vicious taste for reading about works of art instead of reading the works themselves, it may supply opinion instead of educating taste. But *fact* cannot corrupt taste; it can at worst gratify one taste—a taste for history, let us say, or antiquities, or biography—under the illusion that it is assisting another. The real corrupters are those who supply opinion or fancy; and Goethe and Coleridge are not guiltless—for what is Coleridge's *Hamlet*: is it an honest inquiry as far as the data permit, or is it an attempt to present Coleridge in an attractive costume?

[From *The Function of Criticism*. 1923.]

THE EXPERIENCE OF LITERATURE

The author of a work of imagination is trying to affect us wholly, as human beings, whether he knows it or not; and we are affected by it, as human beings, whether we intend to be or not. I suppose that everything we eat has some other effect upon us than merely the pleasure of taste and mastication; it affects us during the process of assimilation and digestion; and I believe that exactly the same is true of anything we read.

The fact that what we read does not concern merely something called our *literary taste*, but that it affects directly, though only amongst many other influences, the whole of what we are, is best elicited, I think, by a conscientious examination of the history of our individual literary education. Consider the adolescent reading of any person with some literary sensibility. Everyone, I believe, who is at all sensible to the seductions of poetry, can remember some moment in youth when he or she was completely carried away by the work of one poet. Very likely he was carried away by several poets, one after the other. The reason for this passing infatuation is not merely that our sensibility to poetry is keener in adolsecence than in maturity. What happens is a kind of inundation, of invasion of the undeveloped personality, the empty (swept and garnished) room, by the stronger personality of the poet. The same thing may happen at a later age to persons who have not done much reading. One author takes complete possession of us for a time; then another; and finally they begin to affect each other in our mind. We weigh one against another; we see that each has qualities absent from others, and qualities incompatible with the qualities of others: we begin to be, in fact, critical; and it is our growing critical power which protects us from excessive possession by any one literary personality. The good critic—and we should all try to be critics, and not leave criticism to the fellows who write reviews in the papers—is the man who, to a keen and abiding sensibility, joins wide and increasingly discriminating reading. Wide reading is not valuable as a kind of hoarding, an accumulation of knowledge, or what sometimes is meant by the term "a well-stocked mind". It is valuable because in the process of being affected by one powerful personality after another, we cease to be dominated by any one, or by any small number. The very different views of life, cohabiting in our minds, affect each other, and our own personality asserts itself and gives each a place in some arrangement peculiar to ourself.

It is simply not true that works of fiction, prose or verse, that is to say works depicting the actions, thoughts, and words and passions of imaginary human beings, *directly* extend our knowledge of life.

Direct knowledge of life is knowledge directly in relation to ourselves, it is our knowledge of *how* people behave in general, of *what* they are like in general, in so far as that part of life in which we ourselves have participated gives us material for generalization. Knowledge of life obtained through fiction is only possible by another stage of self-consciousness. That is to say, it can only be a knowledge of other people's knowledge of life, not of life itself. So far as we are taken up with the happenings in any novel in the same way in which we are taken up with what happens under our eyes, we are acquiring at least as much falsehood as truth. But when we are developed enough to say: "This is the view of life of a person who was a good observer within his limits, Dickens, or Thackeray, or George Eliot, or Balzac; but he looked at it in a different way from me, because he was a different man; he even selected rather different things to look at, or the same things in a different order of importance, because he was a different man; so what I am looking at is the world as seen by a particular mind"—then we are in a position to gain something from reading fiction. We are learning *something* about life from these authors direct, just as we learn something from the reading of history direct; but these authors are only really helping us when we can see, and allow for, their differences from ourselves.

Now what we get, as we gradually grow up and read more and more, and read a greater diversity of authors, is a variety of views of life. But what people commonly assume, I suspect, is that we gain this experience of other men's views of life only by "improving reading". This, it is supposed, is a reward we get by applying ourselves to Shakespeare, and Dante, and Goethe, and Emerson, and Carlyle, and dozens of other respectable writers. The rest of our reading for amusement is merely killing time. But I incline to come to the alarming conclusion that it is just the literature that we read for "amusement", or "purely for pleasure" that may have the greatest, and least suspected influence upon us. It is the literature which we read with the least effort that can have the easiest and most insidious influence upon us. Hence it is that the influence of popular novelists, and of popular plays of contemporary life, requires to be scrutinized most closely. And it is chiefly *contemporary* literature that the majority of people ever read in this attitude of "purely for pleasure", of pure passivity.

[From *Religion and Literature*. 1934.]

TRADITION

❧

Tradition is not solely, or even primarily, the maintenance of certain dogmatic beliefs; these beliefs have come to take their living form in the course of the formation of a tradition. What I mean by tradition involves all those habitual actions, habits, and customs, from the most significant religious rite to our conventional way of greeting a stranger, which represent the blood kinship of "the same people living in the same place". It involves a good deal which can be called *taboo*: that this word is used in our time in an exclusively derogatory sense is to me a curiosity of some significance. We become conscious of these items, or conscious of their importance, usually only after they have begun to fall into desuetude, as we are aware of the leaves of a tree when the autumn wind begins to blow them off—when they have separately ceased to be vital. Energy may be wasted at that point in a frantic endeavour to collect the leaves as they fall and gum them onto the branches: but the sound tree will put forth new leaves, and the dry tree should be put to the axe. We are always in danger, in clinging to an old tradition, or attempting to re-establish one, of confusing the vital and the unessential, the real and the sentimental. Our second danger is to associate tradition with the immovable; to think of it as something hostile to all change; to aim to return to some previous condition which we imagine as having been capable of preservation in perpetuity, instead of aiming to stimulate the life which produced that condition in its time.

It is not of advantage to us to indulge a sentimental attitude towards the past. For one thing, in even the very best living tradition there is always a mixture of good and bad, and much that deserves criticism; and for another, tradition is not a matter of feeling alone. Nor can we safely, without very critical examination, dig ourselves in stubbornly to a few dogmatic notions, for what is a healthy belief at one time may, unless it is one of the few fundamental things, be a pernicious prejudice at another. Nor should we cling to traditions as a way of asserting our superiority over less favoured peoples. What we can do is to use our minds, remembering that a tradition without intelligence is not worth having, to discover what is the best life for us not as a political abstraction, but as a particular people in a particular place; what in the past is worth preserving and what should be rejected; and what conditions, within our power to bring about, would foster the society that we desire.

[From *After Strange Gods*. 1933.]

TRADITION AND THE INDIVIDUAL TALENT

~~~~~

In English writing we seldom speak of tradition, though we occasionally apply its name in deploring its absence. We cannot refer to "the tradition" or to "a tradition"; at most, we employ the adjective in saying that the poetry of So-and-so is "traditional" or even "too traditional". Seldom, perhaps, does the word appear except in a phrase of censure. If otherwise, it is vaguely approbative, with the implication, as to the work approved, of some pleasing archaeological reconstruction. You can hardly make the word agreeable to English ears without this comfortable reference to the reassuring science of archaeology.

Certainly the word is not likely to appear in our appreciations of living or dead writers. Every nation, every race, has not only its own creative, but its own critical turn of mind; and is even more oblivious of the shortcomings and limitations of its critical habits than of those of its creative genius. We know, or think we know, from the enormous mass of critical writing that has appeared in the French language the critical method or habit of the French; we only conclude (we are such unconscious people) that the French are "more critical" than we, and sometimes even plume ourselves a little with the fact, as if the French were the less spontaneous. Perhaps they are; but we might remind ourselves that criticism is as inevitable as breathing, and that we should be none the worse for articulating what passes in our minds when we read a book and feel an emotion about it, for criticizing our own minds in their work of criticism. One of the facts that might come to light in this process is our tendency to insist, when we praise a poet, upon those aspects of his work in which he least resembles anyone else. In these aspects or parts of his work we pretend to find what is individual, what is the peculiar essence of the man. We dwell with satisfaction upon the poet's difference from his predecessors, especially his immediate predecessors; we endeavour to find something that can be isolated in order to be enjoyed. Whereas if we approach a poet without this prejudice we shall often find that not only the best, but the most individual parts of his work may be those in which the dead poets, his ancestors, assert their immortality most vigorously. And I do not mean the impressionable period of adolescence, but the period of full maturity.

Yet if the only form of tradition, of handing down, consisted in following the ways of the immediate generation before us in a blind or timid adherence to its successes, "tradition" should positively be discouraged. We have seen many such simple currents soon lost in the sand; and novelty is better than repetition. Tradition is a matter of much wider significance. It cannot be inherited, and if you want it you must obtain it by great labour. It involves, in the first place, the historical sense, which we may call nearly indispensable to anyone who would continue to be a poet beyond his twenty-fifth year; and the historical sense involves a perception, not only of the pastness of the past, but of its presence; the historical sense compels a man to write not merely with his own generation in his bones, but with a feeling that the whole of the literature of Europe from Homer and within it the whole of the literature of his own country has a simultaneous existence and composes a simultaneous order. This historical sense which is a sense of the timeless as well as of the temporal and of the timeless and of the temporal together, is what makes a writer traditional. And it is at the same time what makes a writer most acutely conscious of his place in time, of his own contemporaneity.

No poet, no artist of any art, has his complete meaning alone. His significance, his appreciation is the appreciation of his relation to the dead poets and artists. You cannot value him alone; you must set him, for contrast and comparison, among the dead. I mean this as a principle of aesthetic, not merely historical, criticism. The necessity that he shall conform, that he shall cohere, is not onesided; what happens when a new work of art is created is something that happens simultaneously to all the works of art which preceded it. The existing monuments form an ideal order among themselves, which is modified by the introduction of the new (the really new) work of art among them. The existing order is complete before the new work arrives; for order to persist after the supervention of novelty, the *whole* existing order must be, if ever so slightly, altered; and so the relations, proportions, values of each work of art towards the whole are readjusted; and this is conformity between the old and the new. Whoever has approved this idea of order, of the form of European, of English literature will not find it preposterous that the past should be altered by the present as much as the present is directed by the past. And the poet who is aware of this will be aware of great difficulties and responsibilities.

In a peculiar sense he will be aware also that he must inevitably be judged by the standards of the past. I say judged, not amputated, by them; not judged to be as good as, or worse or better than, the dead; and certainly not judged by the canons of dead critics. It is a judgement, a comparison, in which two things are measured by each other. To conform merely would be for the new work not really to conform at all; it would not be new, and would therefore not be a work of art. And we do not quite say that the new is more valuable because it fits in; but its fitting in is a test of its value—a test, it is true, which can only be slowly and cautiously applied, for we are none of us infallible judges of conformity. We say: it appears to conform, and is perhaps individual, or it appears individual, and may conform; but we are hardly likely to find that it is one and not the other.

To proceed to a more intelligible exposition of the relation of the poet to the past: he can neither take the past as a lump, an indiscriminate bolus, nor can he form himself wholly on one or two private admirations, nor can he form himself wholly upon one preferred period. The first course is inadmissible, the second is an important experience of youth, and the third is a pleasant and highly desirable supplement. The poet must be very conscious of the main current, which does not at all flow invariably through the most distinguished reputations. He must be quite aware of the obvious fact that art never improves, but that the material of art is never quite the same. He must be aware that the mind of Europe—the mind of his own country—a mind which he learns in time to be much more important than his own private mind—is a mind which changes, and that this change is a development which abandons nothing *en route*, which does not superannuate either Shakespeare, or Homer, or the rock drawing of the Magdalenian draughtsmen. That this development, refinement perhaps, complication certainly, is not, from the point of view of the artist, any improvement. Perhaps not even an improvement from the point of view of the psychologist or not to the extent which we imagine; perhaps only in the end based upon a complication in economics and machinery. But the difference between the present and the past is that the conscious present is an awareness of the past in a way and to an extent which the past's awareness of itself cannot show.

Someone said: "The dead writers are remote from us because we *know* so much more than they did." Precisely, and they are that which we know.

I am alive to a usual objection to what is clearly part of my programme for the *métier* of poetry. The objection is that the doctrine requires a ridiculous amount of erudition (pedantry), a claim which can be rejected by appeal to the lives of poets in any pantheon. It will even be affirmed that much learning deadens or perverts poetic sensibility. While, however, we persist in believing that a poet ought to know as much as will not encroach upon his necessary receptivity and necessary laziness, it is not desirable to confine knowledge to whatever can be put into a useful shape for examinations, drawing-rooms or the still more pretentious modes of publicity. Some can absorb knowledge, the more tardy must sweat for it. Shakespeare acquired more essential history from Plutarch than most men could from the whole British Museum. What is to be insisted upon is that the poet must develop or procure the consciousness of the past and that he should continue to develop this consciousness throughout his career.

What happens is a continual surrender of himself as he is at the moment to something which is more valuable. The progress of an artist is a continual self-sacrifice, a continual extinction of personality.

There remains to define this process of depersonalization and its relation to the sense of tradition. It is in this depersonalization that art may be said to approach the condition of science. I therefore invite you to consider, as a suggestive analogy, the action which takes place when a bit of finely filiated platinum is introduced into a chamber containing oxygen and sulphur dioxide.

II

Honest criticism and sensitive appreciation is directed not upon the poet but upon the poetry. If we attend to the confused cries of the newspaper critics and the susurrus of popular repetition that follows, we shall hear the names of poets in great numbers; if we seek not Blue-book knowledge but the enjoyment of poetry, and ask for a poem, we shall seldom find it. I have tried to point out the importance of the relation of the poem to other poems by other authors, and suggested the conception of poetry as a living whole of all the poetry that has ever been written. The other aspect of this Impersonal theory of poetry is the relation of the poem to its author. And I hinted, by an analogy, that the mind of the mature poet differs from that of the immature one not precisely in any valuation of "personality", not being necessarily more interesting, or having "more to say", but rather by being a more finely perfected medium in which special, or very varied, feelings are at liberty to enter into new combinations.

The analogy was that of the catalyst. When the two gases previously mentioned are mixed in the presence of a filament of platinum, they form sulphurous acid. This combination takes place only if

29

the platinum is present; nevertheless the newly formed acid contains no trace of platinum, and the platinum itself is apparently unaffected: has remained inert, neutral, and unchanged. The mind of the poet is the shred of platinum. It may partly or exclusively operate upon the experience of the man himself; but, the more perfect the artist, the more completely separate in him will be the man who suffers and the mind which creates; the more perfectly will the mind digest and transmute the passions which are its material.

The experience, you will notice, the elements which enter the presence of the transforming catalyst, are of two kinds: emotions and feelings. The effect of a work of art upon the person who enjoys it is an experience different in kind from any experience not of art. It may be formed out of one emotion, or may be a combination of several; and various feelings, inhering for the writer in particular words or phrases or images, may be added to compose the final result. Or great poetry may be made without the direct use of any emotion whatever: composed out of feelings solely. Canto XV of the *Inferno* (Brunetto Latini) is a working up of the emotion evident in the situation; but the effect, though single as that of any work of art, is obtained by considerable complexity of detail. The last quatrain gives an image, a feeling attaching to an image, which "came", which did not develop simply out of what precedes, but which was probably in suspension in the poet's mind until the proper combination arrived for it to add itself to. The poet's mind is in fact a receptacle for seizing and storing up numberless feelings, phrases, images, which remain there until all the particles which can unite to form a new compound are present together.

If you compare several representative passages of the greatest poetry you see how great is the variety of types of combination, and also how completely any semi-ethical criterion of "sublimity" misses the mark. For it is not the "greatness", the intensity, of the emotions, the components, but the intensity of the artistic process, the pressure, so to speak, under which the fusion takes place, that counts. The episode of Paolo and Francesca employs a definite emotion, but the intensity of the poetry is something quite different from whatever intensity in the supposed experience it may give the impression of. It is no more intense, furthermore, than Canto XXVI, the voyage of Ulysses, which has not the direct dependence upon an emotion. Great variety is possible in the process of transmutation of emotion: the murder of Agamemnon, or the agony of Othello, gives an artistic effect apparently closer to a possible original than the scenes from Dante. In the *Agamemnon*, the artistic emotion approximates to the emotion of an actual spectator; in *Othello* to the emotion of the protagonist himself. But the difference between art and the event is always absolute; the combination which is the murder of Agamemnon is probably as complex as that which is the voyage of Ulysses. In either case there has been a fusion of elements. The ode of Keats contains a number of feelings which have nothing particular to do with the nightingale, but which the nightingale, partly perhaps because of its attractive name, and partly because of its reputation, served to bring together.

The point of view which I am struggling to attack is perhaps related to the metaphysical theory of the substantial unity of the soul: for my meaning is, that the poet has, not a "personality" to express, but a particular medium, which is only a medium and not a personality, in which impressions and experiences combine in peculiar and unexpected ways. Impressions and experiences which are important for the man may take no place in the poetry, and those which become important in the poetry may play quite a negligible part in the man, the personality.

I will quote a passage which is unfamiliar enough to be regarded with fresh attention in the light—or darkness—of these observations:

> *And now methinks I could e'en chide myself*
> *For doating on her beauty, though her death*
> *Shall be revenged after no common action.*
> *Does the silkworm expend her yellow labours*
> *For thee? For thee does she undo herself?*
> *Are lordships sold to maintain ladyships*
> *For the poor benefit of a bewildering minute?*
> *Why does yon fellow falsify highways,*
> *And put his life between the judge's lips,*
> *To refine such a thing—keeps horse and men*
> *To beat their valours for her?* . . .

In this passage (as is evident if it is taken in its context) there is a combination of positive and negative emotions: an intensely strong attraction toward beauty and an equally intense fascination by the ugliness which is contrasted with it and which destroys it. This balance of contrasted emotion is in the dramatic situation to which the speech is pertinent, but that situation alone is inadequate to it. This is, so to speak, the structural emotion, provided by the drama. But the whole effect, the dominant note, is due to the fact that a number of floating feelings, having an affinity to this emotion by no means superficially evident, have combined with it to give us a new art emotion.

It is not in his personal emotions, the emotions provoked by particular events in his life, that the poet is in any way remarkable or interesting. His particular emotions may be simple, or crude, or flat. The emotion in his poetry will be a very complex thing, but not with the complexity of the emotions of people who have very complex or unusual emotions in life. One error, in fact, of eccentricity in poetry is to seek for new human emotions to express; and in this search for novelty in the wrong place it discovers the perverse. The business of the poet is not to find new emotions, but to use the ordinary ones and, in working them up into poetry, to express feelings which are not in actual emotions at all. And emotions which he has never experienced will serve his turn as well as those familiar to him. Consequently, we must believe that "emotion recollected in tranquillity" is an inexact formula. For it is neither emotion, nor recollection, nor, without distortion of meaning, tranquillity. It is a concentration, and a new thing resulting from the concentration, of a very great number of experiences which to the practical and active person would not seem to be experiences at all; it is a concentration which does not happen consciously or of deliberation. These experiences are not "recollected", and they finally unite in an atmosphere which is "tranquil" only in that it is a passive attending upon the event. Of course this is not quite the whole story. There is a great deal, in the writing of poetry, which must be conscious and deliberate. In fact, the bad poet is usually unconscious where he ought to be conscious, and conscious where he ought to be unconscious. Both errors tend to make him "personal". Poetry is not a turning loose of emotion, but an escape from emotion; it is not the expression of personality, but an escape from personality. But, of course, only those who have personality and emotions know what it means to want to escape from these things.

[1917.]

POETRY AND PHILOSOPHY

We say, in a vague way, that Shakespeare, or Dante, or Lucretius, is a poet who thinks, and that Swinburne is a poet who does not think, even that Tennyson is a poet who does not think. But what we really mean is not a difference in quality of thought, but a difference in quality of emotion. The poet who "thinks" is merely the poet who can express the emotional equivalent of thought. But he is not necessarily interested in the thought itself. We talk as if thought was precise and emotion was vague. In reality there is precise emotion and there is vague emotion. To express precise emotion requires as great intellectual power as to express precise thought. But by "thinking" I mean something very different from anything that I find in Shakespeare. Champions of Shakespeare as a great philosopher, have a great deal to say about Shakespeare's power of thought, but they fail to show that he thought to any purpose; that he had any coherent view of life, or that he recommended any procedure to follow. "We possess a great deal of evidence", says Wyndham Lewis, "as to what Shakespeare thought of military glory and martial events." Do we? Or rather, did Shakespeare think anything at all? He was occupied with turning human actions into poetry.

I would suggest that none of the plays of Shakespeare has a "meaning", although it would be equally false to say that a play of Shakespeare is meaningless. All great poetry gives the illusion of a view of life. When we enter into the world of Homer or Sophocles, or Virgil, or Dante, or Shakespeare, we incline to believe that we are apprehending something that can be expressed intellectually; for every precise emotion tends towards intellectual formulation.

We are apt to be deluded by the example of Dante. Here, we think, is a poem which represents an exact intellectual system; Dante has a "philosophy", therefore every poet as great as Dante has a philosophy too. Dante had behind him the system of Saint Thomas, to which his poem corresponds point to point. Therefore Shakespeare had behind him Seneca, or Montaigne, or Machiavelli; and if his work does not correspond point to point with any or a composition of these, then it must be that he did a little quiet thinking on his own, and was better than any of these people at their own job. I can see no reason for believing that either Dante or Shakespeare did any thinking on his own. The people who think that Shakespeare thought, are always people who are not engaged in writing poetry, but who are engaged in thinking, and we all like to think that great men were like ourselves. The difference between Shakespeare and Dante is that Dante had one coherent system of thought behind him; but that was just his luck, and from the point of view of poetry is an irrelevant accident. It happened that at Dante's time thought was orderly and strong and beautiful, and that it was concentrated in one man of the greatest genius; Dante's poetry receives a boost which in a sense it does not merit, from the fact that the thought behind it is the thought of a man as great and lovely as Dante himself: Saint Thomas. The thought behind Shakespeare is of men far inferior to Shakespeare himself: hence the alternative errors, first, that as Shakespeare was as great a poet as Dante, he must have supplied, out of his own thinking, the difference in quality between a Saint Thomas and a Montaigne or a Machiavelli or a Seneca, or second, that Shakespeare is inferior to Dante. In truth neither Shakespeare nor Dante did any real thinking—that was not their job; and the relative value of the thought current at their time, the material enforced upon each to use as the vehicle of his feeling, is of no importance. It does not make Dante a greater poet, or mean that we can learn more from Dante than from Shakespeare. We can certainly learn more from Aquinas than from Seneca, but that is quite a different matter. When Dante says

la sua voluntade e nostra pace

it is great poetry, and there is a great philosophy behind it. When Shakespeare says

As flies to wanton boys, are we to the gods;
They kill us for their sport.

it is *equally* great poetry, though the philosophy be-

37

hind it is not great. But the essential is that each expresses, in perfect language, some permanent human impulse. Emotionally, the latter is just as strong, just as true, and just as informative—just as useful and beneficial in the sense in which poetry is useful and beneficial, as the former.

What every poet starts from is his own emotions. And when we get down to these, there is not much to choose between Shakespeare and Dante. Dante's railings, his personal spleen—sometimes thinly disguised under Old Testament prophetic denunciations —his nostalgia, his bitter regrets for past happiness —or for what seems happiness when it is past—and his brave attempts to fabricate something permanent and holy out of his personal animal feelings—as in the *Vita Nuova*—can all be matched out of Shakespeare. Shakespeare, too, was occupied with the struggle—which alone constitutes life for a poet— to transmute his personal and private agonies into something rich and strange, something universal and impersonal. The rage of Dante against Florence, or Pistoia, or what not, the deep surge of Shakespeare's general cynicism and disillusionment, are merely gigantic attempts to metamorphose private failures and disappointments. The great poet, in writing himself, writes his time. Thus Dante, hardly knowing it, became the voice of the thirteenth century; Shakespeare, hardly knowing it, became the representative of the end of the sixteenth century, of a turning point in history. But you can hardly say that Dante believed, or did not believe, the Thomist philosophy; you can hardly say that Shakespeare believed, or did not believe, the mixed and muddled scepticism of the Renaissance. If Shakespeare had written according to a better philosophy, he would have written worse poetry; it was his business to express the greatest emotional intensity of his time, based on whatever his time happened to think. Poetry is not a substitute for philosophy or theology or religion; it has its own function. But as this function is not intellectual but emotional, it cannot be defined adequately in intellectual terms. We can say that it provides "consolation": strange consolation, which is provided equally by writers so different as Dante and Shakespeare.

[From *Shakespeare and the Stoicism of Seneca*. 1927.]

"ROMANTIC" AND "CLASSIC"

Romanticism and classicism are not matters with which creative writers can afford to bother over much, or with which they do, as a rule, in practice greatly concern themselves. It is true that from time to time writers have labelled themselves "romanticists" or "classicists", just as they have from time to time banded themselves together under other names. These names which groups of writers and artists give themselves are the delight of professors and historians of literature, but should not be taken very seriously; their chief value is temporary and political—that, simply, of helping to make the authors known to a contemporary public; and I doubt whether any poet has ever done himself anything but harm by attempting to write as a "romantic" or as a "classicist". No sensible author, in the midst of something that he is trying to write, can stop to consider whether it is going to be romantic or the opposite. At the moment when one writes, one is what one is, and the damage of a lifetime, and of having been born into an unsettled society, cannot be repaired at the moment of composition.

The danger of using terms like "romantic" and

"classic"—this does not, however, give us permission to avoid them altogether—does not spring so much from the confusion caused by those who use these terms about their own work, as from inevitable shifts of meaning in context. We do not mean quite the same thing when we speak of a writer as romantic, as we do when we speak of a literary period as romantic. Furthermore, we may have in mind, on any particular occasion, certain virtues or vices more or less justly associated with one term or the other, and it is doubtful whether there is any total sum of virtues or of vices which may be arrogated to either class. The opportunities for systematic misunderstanding, and for futile controversy, are accordingly almost ideal; and discussion of the subject is generally conducted by excitement of passion and prejudice, rather than by reason. Finally— and this is the most important point—the differences represented by these two terms are not such as can be confined to a purely literary context. In using them, you are ultimately bringing in all human values, and according to your own schemes of valuation.

[From *After Strange Gods*. 1933.]

JOURNALISM AND LITERATURE

The distinction between "journalism" and "literature" is quite futile, unless we are drawing such violent contrast as that between Gibbon's *History* and to-night's evening paper; and such a contrast itself is too violent to have meaning. You cannot, that is, draw any useful distinction between journalism and literature merely in a scale of literary values, as a difference between the well written and the supremely well written: a second-rate novel is not journalism, but it certainly is not literature. The term "journalism" has deteriorated in the last thirty years; and it is particularly fitting, in the present essay, to try to recall it to its more permanent sense. To my thinking, the most accurate as well as most comprehensive definition of the term is to be obtained through considering the state of mind, and the type of mind, concerned in writing what all would concede to be the *best* journalism. There is a type of mind, and I have a very close sympathy with it, which can only turn to writing, or only produce its best writing, under the pressure of an immediate occasion; and it is this type of mind which I propose to treat as the journalist's. The underlying causes may differ: the cause may be an ardent preoccupation with affairs of the day, or it may be (as with myself) inertia or laziness requiring an immediate stimulus, or a habit formed by early necessity of earning small sums quickly. It is not so much that the journalist works on different material from that of other writers, as that he works from a different, no less and often more honourable, motive.

The indignity commonly thrown at the journalist is this, that his work is said to be of only passing interest, intended to make an immediate strong impression, and destined to eternal oblivion after that instant effect has been produced. To say merely this, however, is to overlook the reasons for which writing may be "ephemeral", and the loose application of that adjective itself, as well as the curious accidents which protect a piece of writing from oblivion. Those persons who are drawn by the powerful attraction of Jonathan Swift read and re-read with enchanted delight *The Drapier's Letters*; and these letters are journalism according to my hint of a definition, if anything is. But *The Drapier's Letters* are such an important item now in English letters, so essential to anyone who would be well read in the literature of England, that we ignore the accident by which we still read them. If Swift had never written *Gulliver's Travels*, and if he had not played a striking and dramatic part in political life, and if this amazing madman had not supplemented these claims to permanence by a most interesting private life, what would be the place of *The Drapier's Letters* now? They would be praised now and then by some student of Anglo-Irish history of the epoch who happened by some odd coincidence to have also an exceptional degree of literary acumen; and they would be read by nobody else. The same fate would have overcome the pamphleteering of Defoe, were he not the author of *Robinson Crusoe* and *Moll Flanders*; or the pamphleteering of Samuel Johnson, were he not the hero of Boswell. To turn to another great English writer of quite a different kind, let us suppose that John Henry Newman had not been also the great leader of the English Church whose defection Gladstone described as a "catastrophe"; that he had not played the prominent role in the nineteenth century that he did play; supposing also that the material of his *Apologia* was as defunct as the subject of Wood's halfpence in Ireland, who but a few discerning connoisseurs of style would ever read that book now or a century hence? And the *Apologia* of Newman is as surely journalism as is the journalism of Swift, Defoe, or Johnson.

To quote an example on the opposite side: the *Martin Marprelate* tracts are not, certainly, as fine prose as the best of Swift, Defoe, Johnson, or Newman. They belong to a cruder period. But still they contain some very fine passages indeed, and the whole controversy is on a high literary level. Who reads them now? except a very small number of people, those who interest themselves in the religious squabbles of that epoch, and those who interest themselves in the prose styles of that epoch. They are not considered a part of the necessary education of the cultivated English-speaking person.

Literary style is sometimes assigned almost magical properties, or is credited with being a mysterious preservative for subject-matter which no longer interests. This is far from being absolutely true. Style alone cannot preserve; only good style in conjunction with permanently interesting content can preserve. All other preservation, such as that of Swift's or Defoe's journalism, is due to a happy accident. Every poetry is not immune, though poetry usually concerns itself with simpler and more eternal matters than anything else; for who, except scholars, and except the eccentric few who are born with a sympathy for such work, or others who have deliberately studied themselves into the right appreciation, can now read through the whole of *The Faerie Queene* with delight?

[From *Charles Whibley*. 1931.]

THE APPRECIATION OF POETRY

The rudiment of criticism is the ability to select a good poem and reject a bad poem; and its most severe test is of its ability to select a good *new* poem, to respond properly to a new situation. The experience of poetry, as it develops in the conscious and mature person, is not merely the sum of the experiences of good poems. Education in poetry requires an organization of these experiences. There is not one of us who is born with, or who suddenly acquires at puberty or later, an infallible discrimination and taste. The person whose experience is limited is always liable to be taken in by the sham or the adulterate article; and we see generation after generation of untrained readers being taken in by the sham and the adulterate in its own time—indeed preferring them, for they are more easily assimilable than the genuine article. Yet a very large number of people, I believe, have the native capacity for enjoying *some* good poetry: how much, or how many degrees of capacity may profitably be distinguished, is not part of my present purpose to inquire. It is only the exceptional reader, certainly, who in the course of time comes to classify and compare his experi-

iences, to see one in the light of others; and who, as
his poetic experiences multiply, will be able to understand each more accurately. The element of enjoyment is enlarged into appreciation, which brings a
more intellectual addition to the original intensity of
feeling. It is a second stage in our understanding of
poetry, when we no longer merely select and reject,
but organize. We may even speak of a third stage,
one of reorganization; a stage at which a person already educated in poetry meets with something new
in his own time, and finds a new pattern of poetry
arranging itself in consequence.

[From *The Use of Poetry and the Use of Criticism*.
Introduction. 1932.]

THE CRITIC OF POETRY

~~~~~~

Such writing as Johnson's *Lives of the Poets* and his essay on Shakespeare loses none of its permanence from the consideration that every generation must make its own appraisal of the poetry of the past, in the light of the performance of its contemporaries and immediate predecessors. Criticism of poetry moves between two extremes. On the one hand the critic may busy himself so much with the implications of a poem, or of one poet's work—implications moral, social, religious or other—that the poetry becomes hardly more than a text for a discourse. Such is the tendency of the moralizing critics of the nineteenth century, to which Landor makes a notable exception. Or if you stick too closely to the "poetry" and adopt no attitude towards what the poet has to say, you will tend to evacuate it of all significance. And furthermore there is a philosophic borderline, which you must not transgress too far or too often, if you wish to preserve your standing as a critic, and are not prepared to present yourself as a philosopher, metaphysician, sociologist, or psychologist instead. Johnson, in these respects, is a type of critical integrity. Within his limitations, he is one of the great critics; and he is a great critic partly because he keeps within his limitations. When you know what they are, you know where you are. Considering all the temptations to which one is exposed in judging contemporary writing, all the prejudices which one is tempted to indulge in judging writers of the immediately preceding generation, I view Johnson's *Lives of the Poets* as a masterpiece of the judicial bench. His style is not so formally perfect as that of some other prose writers of his time. It reads often like the writing of a man who is more habituated to talking than to writing; he seems to think aloud, and in short breaths, rather than in the long periods of the historian or the orator. His criticism is as salutary against the dogmatic excesses of the eighteenth century—more indulged in France than in England—as it is against excessive adulation of individual poets with their faults as well as virtues. For Johnson poetry was still poetry, and not another thing. Had he lived a generation later, he would have been obliged to look more deeply into the foundations, and so would have been unable to leave us an example of what criticism ought to be for a civilization which, being settled, has no need, while it lasts, to inquire into the functions of its parts.

[From *The Use of Poetry and the Use of Criticism*:
The Age of Dryden. 1932.]

"DIFFICULT" POETRY

The difficulty of poetry (and modern poetry is supposed to be difficult) may be due to one of several reasons. First, there may be personal causes which make it impossible for a poet to express himself in any way but an obscure way; while this may be regrettable, we should be glad, I think, that the man has been able to express himself at all. Or difficulty may be due just to novelty: we know the ridicule accorded in turn to Wordsworth, Shelley and Keats, Tennyson and Browning—but must remark that Browning was the first to be *called* difficult; hostile critics of the earlier poets found them difficult, but called them silly. Or difficulty may be caused by the reader's having been told, or having suggested to himself, that the poem is going to prove difficult. The ordinary reader, when warned against the obscurity of a poem, is apt to be thrown into a state of consternation very unfavourable to poetic receptivity. Instead of beginning, as he should, in a state of sensitivity, he obfuscates his senses by the desire to be clever and to look very hard for something he doesn't know what—or else by the desire not to be taken in. There is such a thing as stage fright, but what such readers have is pit or gallery fright. The more seasoned reader, he who has reached, in these matters, a state of greater *purity*, does not bother about understanding; not, at least, at first. I know that some of the poetry to which I am most devoted is poetry which I did not understand at first reading; some is poetry which I am not sure I understand yet: for instance, Shakespeare's. And finally, there is the difficulty caused by the author's having left out something which the reader is used to finding; so that the reader, bewildered, gropes about for what is absent, and puzzles his head for a kind of "meaning" which is not there, and is not meant to be there.

The chief use of the "meaning" of a poem, in the ordinary sense, may be (for here again I am speaking of some kinds of poetry and not all) to satisfy one habit of the reader, to keep his mind diverted and quiet, while the poem does its work upon him: much as the imaginary burglar is always provided with a bit of nice meat for the house-dog. This is a normal situation of which I approve. But the minds of all poets do not work that way; some of them, assuming that there are other minds like their own, become impatient of this "meaning" which seems superfluous, and perceive possibilities of intensity through its elimination. I am not asserting that this situation is ideal; only that we must write our poetry as we can, and take it as we find it. It may be that for some periods of society a more relaxed form of writing is right, and for others a more concentrated. I believe that there must be many people who feel, as I do, that the effect of some of the greater nine-teenth-century poets is diminished by their bulk. Who now, for the pure pleasure of it, reads Words-worth, Shelley and Keats even, certainly Browning and Swinburne and most of the French poets of the century—entire? I by no means believe that the "long poem" is a thing of the past; but at least there must be more in it for the length than our grandparents seemed to demand; and for us, any-thing that can be said as well in prose can be said better in prose. And a great deal, in the way of meaning, belongs to prose rather than to poetry. The doctrine of "art for art's sake", a mistaken one, and more advertised than practised, contained this true impulse behind it, that it is a recognition of the error of the poet's trying to do other people's work. But poetry has as much to learn from prose as from other poetry; and I think that an interaction be-tween prose and verse, like the interaction between language and language, is a condition of vitality in literature.

[From *The Use of Poetry and the Use of Criticism*:
Conclusion. 1933.]

POETIC IMAGERY

~~~~~~

Only a part of an author's imagery comes from his reading. It comes from the whole of his sensitive life since early childhood. Why, for all of us, out of all that we have heard, seen, felt, in a lifetime, do certain images recur, charged with emotion, rather than others? The song of one bird, the leap of one fish, at a particular place and time, the scent of one flower, an old woman on a German mountain path, six ruffians seen through an open window playing cards at night at a small French railway junction where there was a water-mill: such memories may have symbolic value, but of what we cannot tell, for they come to represent the depths of feeling into which we cannot peer. We might just as well ask why, when we try to recall visually some period in the past, we find in our memory just the few meagre arbitrarily chosen set of snapshots that we do find there, the faded poor souvenirs of passionate moments.

[From *The Use of Poetry and the Use of Criticism*:
Conclusion. 1933.]

METRICAL INNOVATION

Innovation in metric is not to be measured solely by the width of the deviation from accepted practice. It is a matter of the historical situation: at some moments a more violent change may be necessary than at others. The problem differs at every period. At some times, a violent revolution may be neither possible nor desirable; at such times, a change which may appear very slight, is the change which the important poet will make. The innovation of Pope, after Dryden, may not seem very great; but it is the mark of the master to be able to make small changes which will be highly significant, as at another time to make radical changes, through which poetry will curve back again to its norm.

[From *"In Memoriam"*. 1936.]

AUDITORY IMAGINATION

~~~~~~

What I call the "auditory imagination" is the feeling for syllable and rhythm, penetrating far below the conscious levels of thought and feeling, invigorating every word; sinking to the most primitive and forgotten, returning to the origin and bringing something back, seeking the beginning and the end. It works through meanings, certainly, or not without meanings in the ordinary sense, and fuses the old and obliterated and the trite, the current, and the new and surprising, the most ancient and the most civilized mentality.

[From *The Use of Poetry and the Use of Criticism.*
Matthew Arnold. 1933.]

Part 2

DRAMATIC CRITICISM

POETIC DRAMA

~~~~~~

I

People have tended to think of verse as a restriction upon drama. They think that the emotional range, and the realistic truth, of drama is limited and circumscribed by verse. People were once content with verse in drama, they say, because they were content with a restricted and artificial range of emotion. Only prose can give the full gamut of modern feeling, can correspond to actuality. But is not every dramatic representation artificial? And are we not merely deceiving ourselves when we aim at greater and greater realism? Are we not contenting ourselves with appearances, instead of insisting upon fundamentals? Has human feeling altered much from Aeschylus to ourselves? I maintain the contrary. I say that prose drama is merely a slight by-product of verse drama. The human soul, in intense emotion, strives to express itself in verse. It is not for me, but for the neurologists, to discover why this is so, and why and how feeling and rhythm are related. The tendency, at any rate, of prose drama is to emphasize the ephemeral and superficial; if we want to get at the permanent and universal we tend to express ourselves in verse.

[From *A Dialogue on Dramatic Poetry.* 1928.]

II

It is possible that what distinguishes poetic drama from prosaic drama is a kind of doubleness in the action, as if it took place on two planes at once. In this it is different from allegory, in which the abstraction is something conceived, not something differently felt, and from symbolism (as in the plays of Maeterlinck) in which the tangible world is deliberately diminished—both symbolism and allegory being operations of the conscious planning mind. In poetic drama a certain apparent irrelevance may be the symptom of this doubleness; or the drama has an under-pattern, less manifest than the theatrical one. We sometimes feel, in following the words and behaviour of some of the characters of Dostoevsky, that they are living at once on the plane that we know and on some other plane of reality from which we are shut out: their behaviour does not seem crazy, but rather in conformity with the laws of some world that we cannot perceive.

[From *John Marston.* 1934.]

GREEK DRAMA

⌁⌁⌁

Behind the dialogue of Greek drama we are always conscious of a concrete visual actuality, and behind that of a specific emotional actuality. Behind the drama of words is the drama of action, the timbre of voice and voice, the uplifted hand or tense muscle, and the particular emotion. The spoken play, the words which we read, are symbols, a shorthand, and often, as in the best of Shakespeare, a very abbreviated shorthand indeed, for the acted and felt play, which is always the real thing. The phrase, beautiful as it may be, stands for a greater beauty still. This is merely a particular case of the amazing unity of Greek, the unity of concrete and abstract in philosophy, the unity of thought and feeling, action and speculation, in life.

[From *Seneca in Elizabethan Translation*. 1927.]

THE PATTERN OF SHAKESPEARE

The standard set by Shakespeare is that of a continuous development from first to last, a development in which the choice both of theme and of dramatic and verse technique in each play seems to be determined increasingly by Shakespeare's state of feeling, by the particular stage of his emotional maturity at the time. What is "the whole man" is not simply his greatest or maturest achievement, but the whole pattern formed by the sequence of plays; so that we may say confidently that the full meaning of any one of his plays is not in itself alone, but in that play in the order in which it was written, in its relation to all of Shakespeare's other plays, earlier and later: we must know all of Shakespeare's work in order to know any of it. No other dramatist of the time approaches anywhere near to this perfection of pattern, of pattern superficial and profound; but the measure in which dramatists and poets approximate to this unity in a lifetime's work, is one of the measures of major poetry and drama.

[From *John Ford*. 1932.]

THE UNITY OF SHAKESPEARE

In Elizabethan and Jacobean drama, and even in the
comedy of Congreve and Wycherley, there is almost
no analysis of the particular society of the times, except in so far as it records the rise of the City families, and their ambition to ally themselves with
needy peerages and to acquire country estates. Even
that rise of the City, in *Eastward Hoe* and *Michael-
mas Term*, is treated lightly as a foible of the age,
and not as a symptom of social decay and change. It
is indeed in the lack of this sense of a "changing
world", of corruptions and abuses peculiar to their
own time, that the Elizabethan and Jacobean dramatists are blessed. We feel that they believed in their
own age, in a way in which no nineteenth- or twen-
tieth-century writer of the greatest seriousness has
been able to believe in his age. And accepting their
age, they were in a position to concentrate their attention, to their respective abilities, upon the common characteristics of humanity in all ages, rather
than upon the differences. We can partly criticize
their age through our study of them, but they did not
so criticize it themselves. In the work of Shakespeare
as a whole, there is to be read the profoundest, and

indeed one of the most sombre studies of humanity that has ever been made in poetry; though it is in fact so comprehensive that we cannot qualify it as a whole as either glad or sorry. We recognize the same assumption of permanence in his minor fellows. Dante held it also, and the great Greek dramatists. In periods of unsettlement and change we do not observe this: it was a changing world which met the eyes of Lucian or of Petronius. But in the kind of analysis in which Shakespeare was supreme the other Elizabethan and Jacobean dramatists differed only in degree and in comprehensiveness.

For the age in which Shakespeare lived and the age into which his influence extended after his death, it must be his work, and his work as a whole, that is our criterion. The whole of Shakespeare's work is *one* poem; and it is the poetry of it in this sense, not the poetry of isolated lines and passages or the poetry of the single figures which he created, that matters most. A man might, hypothetically, compose any number of fine passages or even of whole poems which would each give satisfaction, and yet not be a great poet, unless we felt them to be united by one significant, consistent, and developing personality. Shakespeare is the one, among all his contemporaries, who fulfils these conditions; and the nearest to him is Marlowe. Jonson and Chapman have the consistency, but a far lower degree of significant development; Middleton and Webster take a lower place than these; the author of *The Revenger's Tragedy*, whether we call him Tourneur or Middleton or another, accomplishes all that can be accomplished within the limits of a single play. But in all these dramatists there is the essential, as well as the superficies, of poetry; they give the pattern, or we may say the undertone, of the personal emotion, the personal drama, and struggle, which no biography, however full and intimate, could give us; which nothing can give us but our experience of the plays themselves.

[From *John Ford*. 1932.]

BEN JONSON

The immediate appeal of Jonson is to the mind; his emotional tone is not in the single verse, but in the design of the whole. But not many people are capable of discovering for themselves the beauty which is only found after labour; and Jonson's industrious readers have been those whose interest was historical and curious, and those who have thought that in discovering the historical and curious interest they had discovered the artistic value as well. When we say that Jonson requires study, we do not mean study of his classical scholarship or of seventeenth-century manners. We mean intelligent saturation in his work as a whole; we mean that, in order to enjoy him at all, we must get to the centre of his work and his temperament, and that we must see him unbiased by time, as a contemporary. And to see him as a contemporary does not so much require the power of putting ourselves into seventeenth-century London as it requires the power of setting Jonson in our London.

[From *Ben Jonson*. 1919.]

MIDDLETON'S "CHANGELING"

In reading *The Changeling* we may think, till almost the end of the play, that we have been concerned merely with a fantastic Elizabethan morality, and then discover that we are looking on at a dispassionate exposure of fundamental passions of any time and any place. The usual opinion remains the just judgement: *The Changeling* is Middleton's greatest play. The morality of the convention seems to us absurd. To many intelligent readers this play has only an historical interest, and serves only to illustrate the moral taboos of the Elizabethans. The heroine is a young woman who, in order to dispose of a fiancé to whom she is indifferent, so that she may marry the man she loves, accepts the offer of an adventurer to murder the affianced, at the price (as she finds in due course) of becoming the murderer's mistress. Such a plot is, to a modern mind, absurd; and the consequent tragedy seems a fuss about nothing. But *The Changeling* is not merely contingent for its effect upon our acceptance of Elizabethan good form or convention; it is, in fact, no more dependent upon the convention of its epoch than a play like *A Doll's House*. Underneath the convention there is the stratum of truth permanent in human nature. The tragedy of *The Changeling* is an eternal tragedy, as permanent as *Oedipus* or *Antony and Cleopatra*; it is the tragedy of the not naturally bad but irresponsible and undeveloped nature, caught in the consequences of its own action. In every age and in every civilization there are instances of the same thing: the unmoral nature, suddenly trapped in the inexorable toils of morality—of morality not made by man but by Nature—and forced to take the consequences of an act which it had planned light-heartedly. Beatrice is not a moral creature; she becomes moral only by becoming damned. Our conventions are not the same as those which Middleton assumed for his play. But the possibility of that frightful discovery of morality remains permanent.

[From *Thomas Middleton.* 1927.]

Part 3

INDIVIDUAL AUTHORS

DISSOCIATION OF SENSIBILITY

~~~~~~

The poets of the seventeenth century, the successors of the dramatists of the sixteenth, possessed a mechanism of sensibility which could devour any kind of experience. They are simple, artificial, difficult, or fantastic, as their predecessors were; no less nor more than Dante, Guido Cavalcanti, Guinicelli, or Cino. In the seventeenth century a dissociation of sensibility set in, from which we have never recovered; and this dissociation, as is natural, was aggravated by the influence of the two most powerful poets of the century, Milton and Dryden. Each of these men performed certain poetic functions so magnificently well that the magnitude of the effect concealed the absence of others. The language went on and in some respects improved; the best verse of Collins, Gray, Johnson, and even Goldsmith satisfies some of our fastidious demands better than that of Donne or Marvell or King. But while the language became more refined, the feeling became more crude. The feeling, the sensibility, expressed in the *Country Churchyard* (to say nothing of Tennyson and Browning) is cruder than that in the *Coy Mistress*.

The second effect of the influence of Milton and

Dryden followed from the first, and was therefore slow in manifestation. The sentimental age began early in the eighteenth century, and continued. The poets revolted against the ratiocinative, the descriptive; they thought and felt by fits, unbalanced; they reflected. In one or two passages of Shelley's *Triumph of Life*, in the second *Hyperion*, there are traces of a struggle toward unification of sensibility. But Keats and Shelley died, and Tennyson and Browning ruminated.

[From *The Metaphysical Poets*. 1921.]

MARVELL

Out of that high style developed from Marlowe through Jonson (for Shakespeare does not lend himself to these genealogies) the seventeenth century separated two qualities: wit and magniloquence. Neither is as simple or as apprehensible as its name seems to imply, and the two are not in practice antithetical; both are conscious and cultivated, and the mind which cultivates one may cultivate the other. The actual poetry, of Marvell, of Cowley, of Milton, and of others, is a blend in varying proportions. And we must be on guard not to employ the terms with too wide a comprehension; for like the other fluid terms with which literary criticism deals, the meaning alters with the age, and for precision we must rely to some degree upon the literacy and good taste of the reader. The wit of the Caroline poets is not the wit of Shakespeare, and it is not the wit of Dryden, the great master of contempt, or of Pope, the great master of hatred, or of Swift, the great master of disgust. What is meant is some quality which is common to the songs in *Comus* and Cowley's *Anacreontics* and Marvell's *Horatian Ode*. It is more than a technical accomplishment, or the vocabulary

and syntax of an epoch; it is, what we have desig-
nated tentatively as wit, a tough reasonableness beneath the slight lyric grace. You cannot find it in
Shelley or Keats or Wordsworth; you cannot find
more than an echo of it in Landor; still less in Tennyson or Browning; and among contemporaries Mr.
Yeats is an Irishman and Mr. Hardy is a modern
Englishman—that is to say, Mr. Hardy is without it
and Mr. Yeats is outside of the tradition altogether.
On the other hand, as it certainly exists in Lafon-
taine, there is a large part of it in Gautier. And of
the magniloquence, the deliberate exploitation of
the possibilities of magnificence in language which
Milton used and abused, there is also use and even
abuse in the poetry of Baudelaire.

Wit is not a quality that we are accustomed to
associate with "Puritan" literature, with Milton or
with Marvell. But if so, we are at fault partly in our
conception of wit and partly in our generalizations
about the Puritans. And if the wit of Dryden or of
Pope is not the only kind of wit in the language, the
rest is not merely a little merriment or a little levity
or a little impropriety or a little epigram. And, on
the other hand, the sense in which a man like Marvell
is a "Puritan" is restricted. The persons who opposed Charles I and the persons who supported the
Commonwealth were not all of the flock of Zeal-of-
the-land Busy or the United Grand Junction Ebene-
zer Temperance Association. Many of them were
gentlemen of the time who merely believed, with
considerable show of reason, that government by a
Parliament of gentlemen was better than govern-

ment by a Stuart; though they were, to that extent, Liberal Practitioners, they could hardly foresee the tea-meeting and the Dissidence of Dissent. Being men of education and culture, even of travel, some of them were exposed to that spirit of the age which was coming to be the French spirit of the age. This spirit, curiously enough, was quite opposed to the tendencies latent or the forces active in Puritanism; the contest does great damage to the poetry of Milton; Marvell, an active servant of the public, but a lukewarm partisan, and a poet on a smaller scale, is far less injured by it. His line on the statue of Charles II, "It is such a King as no chisel can mend" may be set off against his criticism of the Great Rebellion: "Men . . . ought and might have trusted the King". Marvell, therefore, more a man of the century than a Puritan, speaks more clearly and unequivocally with the voice of his literary age than does Milton.

[From *Andrew Marvell.* 1921.]

BLAKE

If one follows Blake's mind through the several stages of his poetic development it is impossible to regard him as a naïf, a wild man, a wild pet for the supercultivated. The strangeness is evaporated, the peculiarity is seen to be the peculiarity of all great poetry: something which is found (not everywhere) in Homer and Aeschylus and Dante and Villon, and profound and concealed in the work of Shakespeare —and also in another form in Montaigne and in Spinoza. It is merely a peculiar honesty, which, in a world too frightened to be honest, is peculiarly terrifying. It is an honesty against which the whole world conspires, because it is unpleasant. Blake's poetry has the unpleasantness of great poetry. Nothing that can be called morbid or abnormal or perverse, none of the things which exemplify the sickness of an epoch or a fashion, has this quality; only those things which, by some extraordinary labour of simplification, exhibit the essential sickness or strength of the human soul. And this honesty never exists without great technical accomplishment. The question about Blake the man is the question of the circumstances that concurred to permit this honesty in his work, and what circumstances define its limitations. The favouring conditions probably include these two: that, being early apprenticed to a manual occupation, he was not compelled to acquire any other education in literature than he wanted, or to acquire it for any other reason than that he wanted it; and that, being a humble engraver, he had no journalistic-social career open to him.

There was, that is to say, nothing to distract him from his interests or to corrupt these interests: neither the ambitions of parents or wife, nor the standards of society, nor the temptations of success; nor was he exposed to imitation of himself or of anyone else. These circumstances—not his supposed inspired and untaught spontaneity—are what make him innocent.

The *Songs of Innocence and of Experience,* and the poems from the Rossetti manuscript, are the poems of a man with a profound interest in human emotions, and a profound knowledge of them. The emotions are presented in an extremely simplified, abstract form. This form is one illustration of the eternal struggle of art against education, of the literary artist against the continuous deterioration of language.

It is important that the artist should be highly educated in his own art; but his education is one that is hindered rather than helped by the ordinary processes of society which constitute education for the ordinary man. For these processes consist largely in the acquisition of impersonal ideas which obscure

William Blake

what we really are and feel, what we really want, and what really excites our interest. It is of course not the actual information acquired, but the conformity which the accumulation of knowledge is apt to impose, that is harmful. Tennyson is a very fair example of a poet almost wholly encrusted with opinion, almost wholly merged into his environment. Blake, on the other hand, knew what interested him, and he therefore presents only the essential, only, in fact, what can be presented, and need not be explained. And because he was not distracted, or frightened, or occupied in anything but exact statements, he understood. He was naked, and saw man naked, and from the centre of his own crystal. To him there was no more reason why Swedenborg should be absurd than Locke. He accepted Swedenborg, and eventually rejected him, for reasons of his own. He approached everything with a mind unclouded by current opinions. There was nothing of the superior person about him. This makes him terrifying.

We have the same respect for Blake's philosophy (and perhaps for that of Samuel Butler) that we have for an ingenious piece of home-made furniture: we admire the man who has put it together out of the odds and ends about the house. England has produced a fair number of these resourceful Robinson Crusoes; but we are not really so remote from the Continent, or from our own past, as to be deprived of the advantages of culture if we wish them.

We may speculate, for amusement, whether it would not have been beneficial to the north of Europe

78

generally, and to Britain in particular, to have had a more continuous religious history. The local divinities of Italy were not wholly exterminated by Christianity, and they were not reduced to the dwarfish fate which fell upon our trolls and pixies. The latter, with the major Saxon deities, were perhaps no great loss in themselves, but they left an empty place; and perhaps our mythology was further impoverished by the divorce from Rome. Milton's celestial and infernal regions are large but insufficiently furnished apartments filled by heavy conversation; and one remarks about the Puritan mythology its thinness. And about Blake's supernatural territories, as about the supposed ideas that dwell there, we cannot help commenting on a certain meanness of culture. They illustrate the crankiness, the eccentricity, which frequently affects writers outside of the Latin traditions, and which such a critic as Arnold should certainly have rebuked. And they are not essential to Blake's inspiration.

Blake was endowed with a capacity for considerable understanding of human nature, with a remarkable and original sense of language and the music of language, and a gift of hallucinated vision. Had these been controlled by a respect for impersonal reason, for common sense, for the objectivity of science, it would have been better for him. What his genius required, and what it sadly lacked, was a framework of accepted and traditional ideas which would have prevented him from indulging in a philosophy of his own, and concentrated his attention upon the problems of the poet. Confusion of thought, emotion, and vision is what we find in such a work as *Also Sprach Zarathustra*; it is eminently not a Latin virtue. The concentration resulting from a framework of mythology and theology and philosophy is one of the reasons why Dante is a classic, and Blake only a poet of genius. The fault is perhaps not with Blake himself, but with the environment which failed to provide what such a poet needed; perhaps the circumstances compelled him to fabricate, perhaps the poet required the philosopher and mythologist; although the conscious Blake may have been quite unconscious of the motives.

[From *William Blake*. 1920.]

COLERIDGE

Coleridge was one of those unhappy persons—
Donne, I suspect, was such another—of whom one
might say, that if they had not been poets, they
might have made something of their lives, might
even have had a career; or conversely, that if they
had not been interested in so many things, crossed
by such diverse passions, they might have been great
poets. It was better for Coleridge, as poet, to read
books of travel and exploration than to read books
of metaphysics and political economy. He did gen-
uinely want to read books of metaphysics and political economy, for he had a certain talent for such subjects. But for a few years he had been visited by the
Muse (I know of no poet to whom this hackneyed
metaphor is better applicable) and thenceforth was a
haunted man; for anyone who has ever been visited
by the Muse is thenceforth haunted. He had no vocation for the religious life, for there again some-
body like a Muse, or a much higher being, is to be
invoked; he was condemned to know that the little
poetry he had written was worth more than all he
could do with the rest of his life. The author of *Bio-
graphia Litteraria* was already a ruined man. Some-

times, however, to be a "ruined man" is itself a vocation.

[From *The Use of Poetry and the Use of Criticism*: Wordsworth and Coleridge. 1932.]

WORDSWORTH

It would appear that the revolution effected by Wordsworth was very far-reaching indeed. He was not the first poet to present himself as the inspired prophet, nor indeed is this quite Wordsworth's case. Blake may have pretended, and with some claim, to have penetrated mysteries of heaven and hell, but no claim that Blake might make seems to descend upon the "poet" in general; Blake simply had the visions, and made use of poetry to set them forth. Scott, and Byron in his more popular works, were merely society entertainers. Wordsworth is really the first, in the unsettled state of affairs in his time, to annex new authority for the poet, to meddle with social affairs, and to offer a new kind of religious sentiment which it seemed the peculiar prerogative of the poet to interpret. Since Matthew Arnold made his Selections from Wordsworth's poetry, it has become a commonplace to observe that Wordsworth's true greatness as poet is independent of his opinions, of his theory of diction or of his nature-philosophy, and that it is found in poems in which he has no ulterior motive whatever. I am not sure that this critical eclecticism cannot go too far; that we can judge and enjoy a man's poetry while leaving wholly out of account all of the things for which he cared deeply, and on behalf of which he turned his poetry to account. If we dismiss Wordsworth's interests and beliefs, just how much, I wonder, remains? To retain them, or to keep them in mind instead of deliberately extruding them in preparation for enjoying his poetry, is that not necessary to appreciate how great a poet Wordsworth really is? Consider, for instance, one of the very finest poets of the first part of the nineteenth century: Landor. He is an undoubted master of verse and prose; he is the author of at least one long poem which deserves to be much more read than it is; but his reputation has never been such as to bring him into comparison with Wordsworth or with either of the younger poets with whom we have now to deal. It is not only by reason of a handful of poems or a number of isolated lines expressive of deeper emotion than that of which Landor was capable, that we give Wordsworth his place; there is something integral about such greatness, and something significant in his place in the pattern of history, with which we have to reckon. And in estimating for ourselves the greatness of a poet we have to take into account also the *history* of his greatness. Wordsworth is an essential part of history; Landor only a magnificent by-product.

[From *The Use of Poetry and the Use of Criticism*: Shelley and Keats. 1933.]

ARNOLD

＊＊＊＊＊

Arnold was not a man of vast or exact scholarship, and he had neither walked in hell nor been rapt to heaven; but what he did know, of books and men, was in its way well-balanced and well-marshalled. After the prophetic frensies of the end of the eighteenth and the beginning of the nineteenth century, he seems to come to us saying: "This poetry is very fine, it is opulent and careless, it is sometimes profound, it is highly original; but you will never establish and maintain a tradition if you go on in this haphazard way. There are minor virtues which have flourished better at other times and in other countries: these you must give heed to, these you must apply, in your poetry, in your prose, in your conversation and your way of living; else you condemn yourselves to enjoy only fitful and transient bursts of literary brilliance, and you will never, as a people, a nation, a race, have a fully formed tradition and personality." However well-nourished we may be on previous literature and previous culture, we cannot afford to neglect Arnold.

I have elsewhere tried to point out some of Arnold's weaknesses when he ventured into departments of thought for which his mind was unsuited and ill-equipped. In philosophy and theology he was an undergraduate; in religion a Philistine. It is a pleasanter task to define a man's limitations within the field in which he is qualified; for there, the definition of limitation may be at the same time a precision of the writer's excellences. Arnold's poetry has little technical interest. It is academic poetry in the best sense; the best fruit which can issue from the promise shown by the prize-poem. When he is not simply being himself, he is most at ease in a master's gown: *Empedocles on Etna* is one of the finest academic poems ever written. He tried other robes which became him less well; I cannot but think of *Tristram and Iseult* and *The Forsaken Merman* as charades. *Sohrab and Rustum* is a fine piece, but less fine than *Gebir*; and in the classical line Landor with a finer ear, can beat Arnold every time. But Arnold is a poet to whom one readily returns. It is a pleasure, certainly, after associating with the riff-raff of the early part of the century, to be in the company of a man *qui sait se conduire*; but Arnold is something more than an agreeable Professor of Poetry. With all his fastidiousness and superciliousness and officiality, Arnold is more intimate with us than Browning, more intimate than Tennyson ever is except at moments, as in the passionate flights in *In Memoriam*. He is the poet and critic of a period of false stability. All his writing in the kind of *Literature and Dogma* seems to me a valiant attempt to dodge the issue, to mediate between Newman and Huxley; but his poetry, the best of it, is too honest to employ any but his genuine feelings of unrest, loneliness and dissatisfaction. Some of his limitations are manifest enough. In his essay on *The Study of Poetry* he has several paragraphs on Burns, and for an Englishman and an Englishman of his time, Arnold understands Burns very well. Perhaps I have a partiality for small oppressive nationalities like the Scots that makes Arnold's patronizing manner irritate me; and certainly I suspect Arnold of helping to fix the wholly mistaken notion of Burns as a singular untutored English dialect poet, instead of as a decadent representative of a great alien tradition. But he says (taking occasion to rebuke the country in which Burns lived) that "no one can deny that it is of advantage to a poet to deal with a beautiful world"; and this remark strikes me as betraying a limitation. It is an advantage to mankind in general to live in a beautiful world; that no one can doubt. But for the poet is it so important? We mean all sorts of things, I know, by Beauty. But the essential advantage for a poet is not to have a beautiful world with which to deal: it is to be able to see beneath both beauty and ugliness; to see the boredom, and the horror, and the glory.

[From *The Use of Poetry and the Use of Criticism*: Matthew Arnold. 1933.]

WALTER PATER AND "MARIUS THE EPICUREAN"

***

Marius the Epicurean marks indeed one of the phases of the fluctuating relations between religion and culture in England since the Reformation; and for this reason the year 1885 is an important one. Newman, in leaving the Anglican Church, had turned his back upon Oxford. Ruskin, with a genuine sensibility for certain types of art and architecture, succeeded in satisfying his nature by translating everything immediately into terms of morals. The vague religious vapourings of Carlyle, and the sharper, more literate social fury of Ruskin yield before the persuasive sweetness of Arnold. Pater is a new variation.

We are liable to confusion if we call this new variation the "aesthete". Pater was, like the other writers I have just mentioned (except Newman), a moralist. If, as the *Oxford Dictionary* tells us, an aesthete is a "professed appreciator of the beautiful" then there are at least two varieties: those whose profession is most vocal, and those whose appreciation is most professional. If we wish to understand painting, we do not go to Oscar Wilde for help. We have specialists, such as Mr. Berenson, or

Mr. Roger Fry. Even in that part of his work which can only be called literary criticism, Pater is always primarily the moralist. In his essay on Wordsworth he says:

"To treat life in the spirit of art, is to make life a thing in which means and ends are identified: to encourage such treatment, the true moral significance of art and poetry."

That was his notion: to find the "true moral significance of art and poetry". Certainly, a writer may be none the less classified as a moralist, if his moralizing is suspect or perverse. We have to-day a witness in the person of M. André Gide. As always in his imaginary portraits, so frequently in his choice of other writers as the subjects of critical studies, Pater is inclined to emphasize whatever is morbid or associated with physical malady. His admirable study of Coleridge is charged with this attraction.

"More than Childe Harold (he says of Coleridge), more than Werther, more than René himself, Coleridge, by what he did, what he was, and what he failed to do, represents that inexhaustible discontent, languor, and home-sickness, that endless regret, the chords of which ring all through our modern literature."

Thus again in Pascal he emphasizes the malady, with its consequences upon the thought; but we feel that somehow what is important about Pascal has been missed. But it is not that he treats philosophers "in the spirit of art", exactly; for when we read him on Leonardo or Giorgione, we feel that there is the same preoccupation, coming between him and the object as it really is. He is, in his own fashion, moralizing upon Leonardo or Giorgione, on Greek art or on modern poetry. His famous dictum: "Of this wisdom, the poetic passion, the desire of beauty, the love of art for art's sake has most; for art comes to you professing frankly to give nothing but the highest quality to your moments as they pass, and simply for those moments' sake", is itself a theory of ethics; it is concerned not with art but with life. The second half of the sentence is of course demonstrably untrue, or else being true of everything else besides art is meaningless; but it is a serious statement of morals. And the disapproval which greeted this first version of the Conclusion to *The Renaissance* is implicitly a just recognition of that fact. "Art for art's sake" is the offspring of Arnold's Culture; and we can hardly venture to say that it is even a perversion of Arnold's doctrine, considering how very vague and ambiguous that doctrine is.

When religion is in a flourishing state, when the whole mind of society is moderately healthy and in order, there is an easy and natural association between religion and art. Only when religion has been partly retired and confined, when an Arnold can sternly remind us that Culture is wider than Religion, do we get "religious art" and in due course "aesthetic religion". Pater undoubtedly had from childhood a religious bent, naturally to all that was liturgical and ceremonious. Certainly this is a real and important part of religion; and Pater cannot thereby be accused of insincerity and "aestheticism". His attitude must be considered both in relation to

90

his own mental powers and to his moment of time. There were other men like him, but without his gift of style, and such men were among his friends. In the pages of Thomas Wright, Pater, more than most of his devout friends, appears a little absurd. His High Churchmanship is undoubtedly very different from that of Newman, Pusey, and the Tractarians, who, passionate about dogmatic essentials, were singularly indifferent to the sensuous expressions of orthodoxy. It was also dissimilar to that of the priest working in a slum parish. He was "naturally Christian"—but within very narrow limitations, the rest of him was just the cultivated Oxford don and disciple of Arnold, for whom religion was a matter of feeling, and metaphysics not much more. Being incapable of sustained reasoning, he could not take philosophy or theology seriously; just as, being primarily a moralist, he was incapable of seeing any work of art simply as it is.

Marius the Epicurean represents the point of English history at which the repudiation of revealed religion by men of culture and intellectual leadership coincides with a renewed interest in the visual arts. It is Pater's most arduous attempt at a work of literature; for *Plato and Platonism* can be almost dissolved into a series of essays. *Marius* itself is incoherent; its method is a number of fresh starts; its content is a hodge-podge of the learning of the classical don, the impressions of the sensitive holiday visitor to Italy, and a prolonged flirtation with the liturgy.

.   .   .   .

Walter Pater and "Marius the Epicurean"

The true importance of the book, I think, is as a document of one moment in the history of thought and sensibility in the nineteenth century. The dissolution of thought in that age, the isolation of art, philosophy, religion, ethics and literature, is interrupted by various chimerical attempts to effect imperfect syntheses. Religion became morals, religion became art, religion became science or philosophy; various blundering attempts were made at alliances between various branches of thought. Each half-prophet believed that he had the whole truth. The alliances were as detrimental all round as the separations. The right practice of "art for art's sake" saw the devotion of Flaubert or Henry James; Pater is not with these men, but rather with Carlyle and Ruskin and Arnold, if some distance below them. *Marius* is significant chiefly as a reminder that the religion of Carlyle or that of Ruskin or that of Arnold or that of Tennyson or that of Browning, is not enough. It represents, and Pater represents more positively than Coleridge of whom he wrote the words, "that inexhaustible discontent, languor, and home-sickness . . . the chords of which ring all through our modern literature".

[From *Arnold and Pater*. 1930.]

TENNYSON

Tennyson lived in a time which was already acutely time-conscious: a great many things seemed to be happening, railways were being built, discoveries were being made, the face of the world was changing. That was a time busy in keeping up to date. It had, for the most part, no hold on permanent things, on permanent truths about man and god and life and death. The surface of Tennyson stirred about with his time; and he had nothing to which to hold fast except his unique and unerring feeling for the sounds of words. But in this he had something that no one else had. Tennyson's surface, his technical accomplishment, is intimate with his depths: what we most quickly see about Tennyson is that which moves between the surface and the depths, that which is of slight importance. By looking innocently at the surface we are most likely to come to the depths, to the abyss of sorrow. Tennyson is not only a minor Virgil, he is also with Virgil as Dante saw him, a Virgil among the Shades, the saddest of all English poets, among the Great in Limbo, the most instinctive rebel against the society in which he was the most perfect conformist.

[From "*In Memoriam*". 1936.]

THOMAS HARDY

~~~~~

The work of Thomas Hardy represents an interesting example of a powerful personality uncurbed by any institutional attachment or by submission to any objective beliefs: unhampered by any ideas, or even by what sometimes acts as a partial restraint upon inferior writers, the desire to please a large public. He seems to me to have written as nearly for the sake of "self-expression" as a man well can; and the self which he had to express does not strike me as a particularly wholesome or edifying matter of communication. He was indifferent even to the prescripts of good writing: he wrote sometimes overpoweringly well, but always very carelessly; at times his style touches sublimity without ever having passed through the stage of being good. In consequence of his self-absorption, he makes a great deal of landscape; for landscape is a passive creature which lends itself to an author's mood. Landscape is fitted too for the purposes of an author who is interested not at all in men's minds, but only in their emotions; and perhaps only in men as vehicles for emotions. It is only, indeed, in their emotional paroxysms that most of Hardy's characters come alive. This extreme emotionalism seems to me a symptom of decadence; it is a cardinal point of faith in a romantic age, to believe that there is something admirable in violent emotion for its own sake, whatever the emotion or whatever its object. But it is by no means self-evident that human beings are most real when most violently excited; violent physical passions do not in themselves differentiate men from each other, but rather tend to reduce them to the same state; and the passion has significance only in relation to the character and behaviour of the man at other moments of his life and in other contexts. Furthermore, strong passion is only interesting or significant in strong men; those who abandon themselves without resistance to excitements which tend to deprive them of reason, become merely instruments of feeling and lose their humanity; and unless there is moral resistance and conflict there is no meaning. But as the majority is capable neither of strong emotion nor of strong resistance, it always inclines to admire passion for its own sake, unless instructed to the contrary; and, if somewhat deficient in vitality, people imagine passion to be the surest evidence of vitality. This in itself may go towards accounting for Hardy's popularity.

[From *After Strange Gods*. 1933.]

THE PENSÉES OF PASCAL

It might seem that about Blaise Pascal, and about the two works on which his fame is founded, everything that there is to say had been said. The details of his life are as fully known as we can expect to know them; his mathematical and physical discoveries have been treated many times; his religious sentiment and his theological views have been discussed again and again; and his prose style has been analysed by French critics. But Pascal is one of those writers who will be and who must be studied afresh by men in every generation. It is not he who changes, but we who change. It is not our knowledge of him that increases, but our world that alters and our attitudes towards it. The history of human opinions of Pascal and of men of his stature is a part of the history of humanity. That indicates his permanent importance.

The few facts of Pascal's life which need to be recalled in examining the *Pensées*, are as follows. He was born at Clermont in Auvergne, in 1623. His family were people of substance of the upper middle class. His father was a government official, who was able to leave, when he died, a sufficient patrimony to his one son and his two daughters. In 1631 the father moved to Paris, and a few years later took up another government post at Rouen. Wherever he lived, the elder Pascal seems to have mingled with some of the best society, and with men of eminence in science and the arts. Blaise was educated entirely by his father at home. He was exceedingly precocious, indeed excessively precocious, for his application to studies in childhood and adolescence impaired his health and is held responsible for his death at thirty-nine. Prodigious, though not incredible stories are preserved, especially of his precocity in mathematics. His mind was active rather than accumulative; he showed from his earliest years that disposition to find things out for himself, which has characterized the infancy of Clerk Maxwell and other scientists. Of his later discoveries in physics there is no need for mention here; it must only be remembered that he counts as one of the greatest physicists and mathematicians of all time; and that his discoveries were made during the years when most scientists are still apprentices.

The elder Pascal, Etienne, was a sincere Christian. About 1646 he fell in with some representatives of the religious revival within the Church which has become known as Jansenism—after Jansenius, Bishop of Ypres, whose theological work is taken as the origin of the movement. This period is usually spoken of as the movement of Pascal's "first conversion". The word "conversion", however, is too forcible to be applied at this point to Blaise Pascal himself. The family had always been devout, and the younger Pascal, though absorbed in his scientific work, never seems to have been afflicted with infidelity. His attention was then directed, certainly, to religious and theological matters; but the term "conversion" can only be applied to his sisters—the elder, already Madame Périer, and particularly the younger, Jacqueline, who at that time conceived a vocation for the religious life. Pascal himself was by no means disposed to renounce the world. After the death of the father in 1650 Jacqueline, a young woman of remarkable strength and beauty of character, wished to take her vows as a sister of Port-Royal, and for some time her wish remained unfulfilled owing to the opposition of her brother. His objection was on the purely worldly ground that she wished to make over her patrimony to the Order; whereas while she lived with him, their combined resources made it possible for him to live more nearly on a scale of expense congenial to his tastes. He liked, in fact, not only to mix with the best society, but to keep a coach and horses—six horses is the number at one time attributed to his carriage. Though he had no legal power to prevent his sister from disposing of her property as she elected the amiable Jacqueline shrank from doing so without her brother's willing approval. The Mother Superior, Mère Angélique—herself an eminent personage in the history of this religious movement—finally persuaded the young novice to enter the order without the satisfaction of bringing her patrimony with her; but Jacqueline remained so distressed by this situation that her brother finally relented.

So far as is known, the worldly life enjoyed by

Pascal during this period can hardly be qualified as "dissipation", and certainly not as "debauchery". Even gambling may have appealed to him chiefly as affording a study of mathematical probabilities. He appears to have led such a life as any cultivated intellectual man of good position and independent means might lead and consider himself a model of probity and virtue. Not even a love-affair is laid at his door, though he is said to have contemplated marriage. But Jansenism, as represented by the religious society of Port-Royal, was morally a Puritan movement within the Church, and its standards of conduct were at least as severe as those of any Puritanism in England or America. The period of fashionable society, in Pascal's life is, however, of great importance in his development. It enlarged his knowledge of men and refined his tastes; he became a man of the world and never lost what he had learnt; and when he turned his thoughts wholly towards religion, his worldly knowledge was a part of his composition which is essential to the value of his work.

Pascal's interest in society did not distract him from scientific research; nor did this period occupy much space in what is a very short and crowded life. Partly his natural dissatisfaction with such a life, once he had learned all it had to teach him, partly the influence of his saintly sister Jacqueline, partly increasing suffering as his health declined, directed him more and more out of the world and to thoughts of eternity. And in 1654 occurs what is called his "second conversion", but which might be called his conversion simply.

He made a note of his mystical experience, which he kept always about him, and which was found, after his death, sewn into the coat which he was wearing. The experience occurred on the 23rd November 1654, and there is no reason to doubt its genuineness unless we choose to deny all mystical experience. Now, Pascal was not a mystic, and his works are not to be classified amongst mystical writings; but what can only be called mystical experience happens to many men who do not become mystics. The work which he undertook soon after, the *Lettres écrites à un Provincial*, is a masterpiece of religious controversy at the opposite pole from mysticism. We know quite well that he was at the time when he received his illumination from God in extremely poor health; but it is a commonplace that some forms of illness are extremely favourable, not only to religious illumination, but to artistic and literary composition. A piece of writing meditated, apparently without progress, for months or years, may suddenly take shape and word; and in this state long passages may be produced which require little or no retouch. I have no good word to say for the cultivation of automatic writing as the model of literary composition; I doubt whether these moments *can* be cultivated by the writer; but he to whom this happens assuredly has the sensation of being a vehicle rather than a maker. No masterpiece can be produced whole by such means: but neither does even the higher form of religious inspiration suffice for the religious life; even the most exalted mystic must return to the world, and use his reason to employ the results of his experience in daily life. You may call it communion with the Divine, or you may call it a temporary crystallization of the mind. Until science can teach us to reproduce such phenomena at will, science cannot claim to have explained them; and they can be judged only by their fruits.

From that time until his death, Pascal was closely associated with the society of Port-Royal which his sister Jacqueline, who predeceased him, had joined as a *religieuse*; the society was then fighting for its life against the Jesuits. Five propositions, judged by a committee of cardinals and theologians at Rome to be heretical, were found to be put forward in the work of Jansenius; and the society of Port-Royal, the representative of Jansenism among communities, suffered a blow from which it never revived. It is not the place here to review the bitter controversy and conflict; the best account, from the point of view of a critic of genius who took no side, who was neither Jansenist nor Jesuit, Christian nor infidel, is that in the great book of Sainte-Beuve, *Port-Royal*. And in this book the parts devoted to Pascal himself are among the most brilliant pages of criticism that Sainte-Beuve ever wrote. It is sufficient to notice that the next occupation of Pascal, after his conversion, was to write these eighteen "Letters", which as prose are of capital importance in the foundation of French classical style, and which as polemic are surpassed by none, not by Demosthenes, or Cicero, or Swift. They have the limitation of all polemic and forensic: they persuade, they seduce, they are unfair. But it is also unfair to assert that, in these *Letters to a Provincial*, Pascal was attacking the Society of Jesus in itself. He was attacking rather a particular school of casuistry which relaxed the requirements of the Confessional; a school which certainly flourished amongst the Society of Jesus, at that time, and of which the Spaniards Escobar and Molina are the most eminent authorities. He undoubtedly abused the art of quotation, as a polemical writer is likely to do; but there were abuses for him to abuse; and he did the job thoroughly. His *Letters* must not be called theology. Academic theology was not a department in which Pascal was versed; when necessary, the fathers of Port-Royal came to his aid. The *Letters* are the work of one of the finest mathematical minds of any time, and of a man of the world who addressed, not theologians, but the world in general —all of the cultivated and many of the less cultivated of the French laity; and with this public they made an astonishing success.

During this time Pascal never wholly abandoned his scientific interests. Though in his religious writings he composed slowly and painfully, and revised often, in matters of mathematics his mind seemed to move with consummate natural ease and grace. Discoveries and inventions sprang from his brain without effort; among the minor devices of this later period, the first omnibus service in Paris is said to owe its origin to his inventiveness. But rapidly failing health, and absorption in the great work he had in mind, left him little time and energy during the last two years of his life.

The plan of what we call the *Pensées* formed itself about 1660. The completed book was to have been a carefully constructed defence of Christianity, a true Apology and a kind of Grammar of Assent, setting forth the reasons which will convince the intellect. As I have indicated before, Pascal was not a theologian, and on dogmatic theology had recourse to his spiritual advisers. Nor was he indeed a systematic philosopher. He was a man with an immense genius for science, and at the same time a natural psychologist and moralist. As he was a great literary artist, his book would have been also his own spiritual autobiography; his style, free from all diminishing idiosyncrasies, was yet very personal. Above all, he was a man of strong passions; and his intellectual passion for truth was reinforced by his passionate dissatisfaction with human life unless a spiritual explanation could be found.

We must regard the *Pensées* as merely the first notes for a work which he left far from completion; we have, in Sainte-Beuve's words, a tower of which the stones have been laid on each other, but not cemented, and the structure unfinished. In early years his memory had been amazingly retentive of anything that he wished to remember; and had it not been impaired by increasing illness and pain, he probably would not have been obliged to set down these notes at all. But taking the book as it is left to us, we still find that it occupies a unique place in the history of French literature and in the history of religious meditation.

To understand the method which Pascal employs,

the reader must be prepared to follow the process of the mind of the intelligent believer. The Christian thinker—and I mean the man who is trying consciously and conscientiously to explain to himself the sequence which culminates in faith, rather than the public apologist—proceeds by rejection and elimination. He finds the world to be so and so; he finds its character inexplicable by any non-religious theory: among religions he finds Christianity, and Catholic Christianity, to account most satisfactorily for the world and especially for the moral world within; and thus, by what Newman calls "powerful and concurrent" reasons, he finds himself inexorably committed to the dogma of the Incarnation. To the unbeliever, this method seems disingenuous and perverse: for the unbeliever is, as a rule, not so greatly troubled to explain the world to himself, nor so greatly distressed by its disorder; nor is he generally concerned (in modern terms) to "preserve values". He does not consider that if certain emotional states, certain development of character, and what in the highest sense can be called "saintliness" are inherently and by inspection known to be good, then the satisfactory explanation of the world must be an explanation which will admit the "reality" of these values. Nor does he consider such reasoning admissible; he would, so to speak, trim his values according to his cloth, because to him such values are of no great value. The unbeliever starts from the other end, and as likely as not with the question: Is a case of human parthenogenesis credible? and this he would call going straight to the heart of the matter. Now

Pascal's method is, on the whole, the method natural and right for the Christian; and the opposite method is that taken by Voltaire. It is worth while to remember that Voltaire, in his attempt to refute Pascal, has given once and for all the type of such refutation; and that later opponents of Pascal's Apology for the Christian Faith have contributed little beyond psychological irrelevancies. For Voltaire has presented, better than anyone since, what is the unbelieving point of view; and in the end we must all choose for ourselves between one point of view and another.

I have said above that Pascal's method is "on the whole" that of the typical Christian apologist; and this reservation was directed at Pascal's belief in miracles, which plays a larger part in his construction than it would in that, at least, of the modern Catholic. It would seem fantastic to accept Christianity because we first believe the Gospel miracles to be true, and it would seem impious to accept it primarily because we believe more recent miracles to be true; we accept the miracles, or some miracles, to be true because we believe the Gospel of Jesus Christ: we found our belief in the miracles on the Gospel, not our belief in the Gospel on the miracles. But it must be remembered that Pascal had been deeply impressed by a contemporary miracle, known as the miracle of the Holy Thorn: a thorn reputed to have been preserved from the Crown of Our Lord was pressed upon an ulcer which quickly healed. Sainte-Beuve, who as a medical man felt himself on solid ground, discusses fully the possible explanation of this apparent miracle. It is true that the miracle happened at Port-Royal, and that it arrived opportunely to revive the depressed spirits of the community in its political afflictions; and it is likely that Pascal was the more inclined to believe a miracle which was performed upon his beloved sister. In any case, it probably led him to assign a place to miracles in his study of faith, which is not quite that which we should give to them ourselves.

Now the great adversary against whom Pascal set himself, from the time of his first conversations with M. de Saci at Port-Royal, was Montaigne. One cannot destroy Pascal, certainly; but of all authors Montaigne is one of the least destructible. You could as well dissipate a fog by flinging hand-grenades into it. For Montaigne is a fog, a gas, a fluid, insidious element. He does not reason, he insinuates, charms, and influences; or if he reasons, you must be prepared for his having some other design upon you than to convince you by his argument. It is hardly too much to say that Montaigne is the most essential author to know, if we would understand the course of French thought during the last three hundred years. In every way, the influence of Montaigne was repugnant to the men of Port-Royal. Pascal studied him with the intention of demolishing him. Yet, in the *Pensées*, at the very end of his life, we find passage after passage and the slighter they are the more significant, almost "lifted" out of Montaigne, down to a figure of speech or a word. The parallels are most often with the long essay of Montaigne called *L'Apologie de Ray-*

106

mond Sébond—an astonishing piece of writing upon which Shakespeare also probably drew in *Hamlet*. Indeed, by the time a man knew Montaigne well enough to attack him, he would already be thoroughly infected by him.

It would, however, be grossly unfair to Pascal, to Montaigne, and indeed to French literature, to leave the matter at that. It is no diminution of Pascal, but only an aggrandizement of Montaigne. Had Montaigne been an ordinary life-sized sceptic, a small man like Anatole France, or even a greater man like Renan, or even like the greatest sceptic of all, Voltaire, this "influence" would be to the discredit of Pascal; but if Montaigne had been no more than Voltaire, he could not have affected Pascal at all. The picture of Montaigne which offers itself first to our eyes, that of the original and independent solitary "personality", absorbed in amused analysis of himself, is deceptive. Montaigne's is no *limited* Pyrrhonism, like that of Voltaire, Renan, or France. He exists, so to speak, on a plane of numerous concentric circles, the most apparent of which is the small inmost circle, a personal puckish scepticism which can be easily aped if not imitated. But what makes Montaigne a very great figure is that he succeeded, God knows how—for Montaigne very likely did not know that he had done it—it is not the sort of thing that men *can* observe about themselves, for it is essentially bigger than the individual's consciousness —he succeeded in giving expression to the scepticism of *every* human being. For every man who thinks and lives by thought must have his own scepticism, that which stops at the question, that which ends in denial, or that which leads to faith and which is somehow integrated into the faith which transcends it. And Pascal, as the type of one kind of religious believer, which is highly passionate and ardent but passionate only through a powerful and regulated intellect, is in the first sections of his unfinished Apology for Christianity facing unflinchingly the demon of doubt which is inseparable from the spirit of belief.

There is accordingly something quite different from an influence which would prove Pascal's weakness; there is a real affinity between his doubt and that of Montaigne; and through the common kinship with Montaigne Pascal is related to the noble and distinguished line of French moralists, from La Rochefoucauld down. In the honesty with which they face the *données* of the actual world this French tradition has a unique quality in European literature, and in the seventeenth century Hobbes is crude in comparison.

Pascal is a man of the world among ascetics, and an ascetic among men of the world; he had the knowledge of worldliness and the passion of asceticism, and in him the two are fused into an individual whole. The majority of mankind is lazy-minded, incurious, absorbed in vanities, and tepid in emotion, and is therefore incapable of either much doubt or much faith; and when the ordinary man calls himself a sceptic or an unbeliever, that is ordinarily a simple pose, cloaking a disinclination to think anything out to a conclusion. Pascal's disillusioned analysis of human bondage is sometimes interpreted to mean that Pascal was really and finally an un-believer, who, in his despair, was incapable of en-during reality and enjoying the heroic satisfaction of the free man's worship of nothing. His despair, his disillusion, are, however, no illustration of personal weakness; they are perfectly objective, because they are essential moments in the progress of the intel-lectual soul; and for the type of Pascal they are the analogue of the drought, the dark night, which is an essential stage in the progress of the Christian mys-tic. A similar despair, when it is arrived at by a diseased character or an impure soul, may issue in the most disastrous consequences though with the most superb manifestations; and thus we get *Gulli-ver's Travels*; but in Pascal we find no such distor-tion; his despair is in itself more terrible than Swift's, because our heart tells us that it corresponds exactly to the facts and cannot be dismissed as men-tal disease; but it was also a despair which was a necessary prelude to, and element in, the joy of faith.

I do not wish to enter any further than necessary upon the question of the heterodoxy of Jansenism; and it is no concern of this essay whether the Five Propositions condemned at Rome were really main-tained by Jansenius in his book *Augustinus*, or whe-ther we should deplore or approve the consequent decay (indeed with some persecution) of Port-Royal. It is impossible to discuss the matter without be-coming involved as a controversialist either for or against Rome. But in a man of the type of Pascal—

and the type always exists—there is, I think, an ingredient of what may be called Jansenism of temperament, without identifying it with the Jansenism of Jansenius and of other devout and sincere, but not immensely gifted doctors. It is accordingly needful to state in brief what the dangerous doctrine of Jansenius was, without advancing too far into theological refinements. It is recognized in Christian theology—and indeed on a lower plane it is recognized by all men in affairs of daily life—that freewill of the natural effort and ability of the individual man and also supernatural *grace*, a gift accorded we know not quite how, are both required, in co-operation, for salvation. Though numerous theologians have set their wits at the problem, it ends in a mystery which we can perceive but not finally decipher. At least, it is obvious that, like any doctrine a slight excess or deviation to one side or the other will precipitate a heresy. The Pelagians, who were refuted by Saint Augustine, emphasized the efficacy of human effort and belittled the importance of supernatural grace. The Calvinists emphasized the degradation of man through Original Sin, and considered mankind so corrupt that the will was of no avail; and thus fell into the doctrine of predestination. It was upon the doctrine of grace according to Saint Augustine that the Jansenists relied; and the *Augustinus* of Jansenius was presented as a sound exposition of the Augustinian views.

Heresies are never antiquated, because they forever assume new forms. For instance, the insistence upon good works and "service" which is preached from many quarters, or the simple faith that anyone who lives a good and useful life need have no "morbid" anxieties about salvation, is a form of Pelagianism. On the other hand, one sometimes hears enounced the view that it will make no real difference if all the traditional religious sanctions for moral behaviour break down, because those who are born and bred to be nice people will always prefer to behave nicely, and those who are not will behave otherwise in any case: and this is surely a form of predestination—for the hazard of being born a nice person or not is as uncertain as the gift of grace.

It is likely that Pascal was attracted as much by the fruits of Jansenism in the life of Port-Royal as by the doctrine itself. This devout, ascetic, thoroughgoing society, striving heroically in the midst of a relaxed and easy-going Christianity, was formed to attract a nature so concentrated, so passionate, and so thoroughgoing as Pascal's. But the insistence upon the degraded and helpless state of man, in Jansenism, is something also to which we must be grateful, for to it we owe the magnificent analysis of human motives and occupations which was to have constituted the early part of his book. And apart from the Jansenism which is the work of a not very eminent bishop who wrote a Latin treatise which is now unread, there is also, so to speak, a Jansenism of the individual biography. A moment of Jansenism may naturally take place, and take place rightly, in the individual; particularly in the life of a man of great and intense intellectual powers, who cannot avoid seeing through human beings and observing the

111

vanity of their thoughts and of their avocations,
their dishonesty and self-deception, the insincerity
of their emotions, their cowardice, the pettiness of
their real ambitions.[1] Actually, considering that much
greater maturity is required for these qualities than
for any mathematical or scientific greatness, how
easily his brooding on *the misery of man without God*
might have encouraged in him the sin of spiritual
pride, the *concupiscence de l'esprit*: and how fast a hold
he has of humility!

And although Pascal brings to his work the same
powers which he exerted in science, it is not as a
scientist that he presents himself. He does not seem
to say to the reader: I am one of the most distinguished scientists of the day: I understand many matters which will always be mysteries to you, and
through science I have come to the Faith; you therefore who are not initiated into science ought to have
faith if I have it. He is fully aware of the difference
of subject-matter; and his famous distinction between the *esprit de géométrie* and the *esprit de finesse*
is one to ponder over.

*En l'un, les principes sont palpables, mais éloignés de
l'usage commun; de sorte qu'on a peine à tourner la tête*

[1] Cette négligence en une affaire où il s'agit d'eux-
memes, de leur éternité, de leur tout, m'irrite plus qu'elle
ne m'attendrit; elle m'étonne et m'épouvante, c'est un
monstre pour moi. Je ne dis pas ceci par le zèle pieux d'une
dévotion spirituelle. J'entends au contraire qu'on doit
avoir ce sentiment par un principe d'intérêt humain et par
un intérêt d'amour-propre: il ne faut pour cela que voir ce
que voient les personnes les moins éclairées. (*Pensées:* ed.
Massis, p. 29.)

de ce côté-là, manque d'habitude: mais pour peu qu'on l'y tourne, on voit les principes à plein; et il faudrait avoir tout à fait l'esprit faux pour mal raisonner sur des principes si gros qu'il est presque impossible qu'ils échappent.

Mais dans l'esprit de finesse, les principes sont dans l'usage commun et devant les yeux de tout le monde. On n'a que faire de tourner la tête, ni de se faire violence; il n'est question que d'avoir bonne vue, mais il faut l'avoir bonne; car les principes sont si déliés et en si grand nombre, qu'il est presque impossible qu'il n'en échappe. Or, l'omission d'un principe mène à l'erreur; ainsi, il faut avoir la vue bien nette pour tous les principes, et ensuite l'esprit juste pour ne pas raisonner faussement sur des principes connus.

It is the just combination of the scientist, the *honnête homme*, and the religious nature with a passionate craving for God, that makes Pascal unique. He succeeds where Descartes fails; for in Descartes the element of *esprit de géométrie* is excessive. And in a few phrases about Descartes, in the present book, Pascal laid his finger on the place of weakness.

Je ne puis pardonner à Descartes; il aurait bien voulu, dans toute sa philosophie, se pouvoir passer de Dieu; mais il n'a pu s'empêcher de lui faire donner une chiquenaude, pour mettre le monde en mouvement; après cela, il n'a plus que faire de Dieu.

He who reads this book will observe at once its fragmentary nature; but only after some study will perceive that the fragmentariness lies in the expression more than in the thought. The "thoughts" cannot be detached from each other and quoted as if each were complete in itself. *Le cœur a ses raisons que la raison ne connait point,* how often one has heard that quoted, and quoted often to the wrong purpose![1] For this is by no means an exaltation of the "heart" over the "head", a defence of unreason. The heart, in Pascal's terminology, is itself truly rational if it is truly the heart. For him, in theological matters which seemed to him much larger, more difficult, and more important than scientific matters, the whole personality is involved.

We cannot quite understand any of the parts, fragmentary as they are, without some understanding of the whole. Capital, for instance, is his analysis of the *three orders*: the order of nature, the order of mind, and the order of charity. These three are *discontinuous*; the higher is not implicit in the lower as in an evolutionary doctrine it would be. In this distinction Pascal offers much about which the modern world would do well to think. And indeed, because of his unique combination and balance of qualities, I know of no religious writer more pertinent to our time. The great mystics, like Saint John of the Cross, are primarily for readers with a special determination of purpose; the devotional writers, such as Saint François de Sales, are primarily for those who already feel consciously desirous of the love of God; the great theologians are for those interested in theology. But I can think of no Christian writer, not Newman even, more to be commended than Pascal

[1] And those who have quoted *C'est là ma place au soleil* have often forgotten to add *Voilà le commencement et l'imvge de l'usurpation de toute la terre.*

to those who doubt, but who have the mind to conceive, and the sensibility to feel, the disorder, the futility, the meaninglessness, the mystery of life and suffering, and who can only find peace through a satisfaction of the whole being.

[1931.]

BAUDELAIRE

~~~~~

I

It was once the mode to take Baudelaire's Satanism seriously, as it is now the tendency to present Baudelaire as a serious and Catholic Christian. Especially as a prelude to the *Journaux Intimes* this diversity of opinion needs some discussion. I think that the latter view—that Baudelaire is essentially Christian—is nearer the truth than the former, but it needs considerable reservation. When Baudelaire's Satanism is dissociated from its less creditable paraphernalia, it amounts to a dim intuition of a part, but a very important part, of Christianity. Satanism itself, so far as not merely an affectation, was an attempt to get into Christianity by the back door. Genuine blasphemy, genuine in spirit and not purely verbal, is the product of partial belief, and is as impossible to the complete atheist as to the perfect Christian. It is a way of affirming belief. This state of partial belief is manifest throughout the *Journaux Intimes*. What is significant about Baudelaire is his theological innocence. He is discovering Christianity for himself; he is not assuming it as a fashion or weighing social or political reasons, or any other accidents. He is beginning, in a way, at the beginning; and, being a discoverer, is not altogether certain what he is exploring and to what it leads; he might almost be said to be making again, as one man, the effort of scores of generations. His Christianity is rudimentary or embryonic; at best, he has the excesses of a Tertullian (and even Tertullian is not considered wholly orthodox and well balanced). His business was not to practise Christianity, but—what was much more important for his time—to assert its *necessity*.

Baudelaire's morbidity of temperament cannot, of course, be ignored: and no one who has looked at the work of Crépet or the recent small biographical study of François Porché can forget it. We should be misguided if we treated it as an unfortunate ailment which can be discounted or attempted to detach the sound from the unsound in his work. Without the morbidity none of his work would be possible or significant; his weaknesses can be composed into a larger whole of strength, and this is implied in my assertion that neither the health of Goethe nor the malady of Baudelaire matters in itself: it is what both men made of their endowments that matters. To the eye of the world, and quite properly for all questions of private life, Baudelaire was thoroughly perverse and insufferable: a man with a talent for ingratitude and unsociability, intolerably irritable, and with a mulish determination to make the worst of everything; if he had money, to squander it; if he had friends, to alienate them; if he had any good fortune, to disdain it. He had the pride of the man who feels in himself great weakness and great strength. Having great genius, he had neither the patience nor the inclination, had he had the power, to overcome his weakness; on the contrary, he exploited it for theoretical purposes. The morality of such a course may be a matter for endless dispute; for Baudelaire, it was the way to liberate his mind and give us the legacy and lesson that he has left.

He was one of those who have great strength, but strength merely to *suffer*. He could not escape suffering and could not transcend it, so he *attracted* pain to himself. But what he could do, with that immense passive strength and sensibilities which no pain could impair, was to study his suffering. And in this limitation he is wholly unlike Dante, not even like any character in Dante's Hell. But, on the other hand, such suffering as Baudelaire's implies the possibility of a positive state of beatitude. Indeed, in his way of suffering is already a kind of presence of the supernatural and of the superhuman. He rejects always the purely natural and the purely human; in other words, he is neither "naturalist" nor "humanist". Either because he cannot adjust himself to the actual world he has to reject it in favour of Heaven and Hell, or because he has the perception of Heaven and Hell he rejects the present world: both ways of putting it are tenable. There is in his statements a good deal of romantic detritus; *ses ailes de géant l'empêchent de marcher*, he says of the Poet and of the Albatross, but not convincingly; but there is also truth about himself and about the world. His *ennui* may of course be explained, as everything can be explained in psychological or pathological terms; but it is also, from the opposite point of view, a true form of *acedia*, arising from the unsuccessful struggle towards the spiritual life.

II

From the poems alone, I venture to think, we are not likely to grasp what seems to me the true sense and significance of Baudelaire's mind. Their excellence of form, their perfection of phrasing, and their superficial coherence, may give them the appearance of presenting a definite and final state of mind. In reality, they seem to me to have the external but not the internal form of classic art. One might even hazard the conjecture that the care for perfection of form, among some of the romantic poets of the nineteenth century, was an effort to support, or to conceal from view, an inner disorder. Now the true claim of Baudelaire as an artist is not that he found a superficial form, but that he was searching for a form of life. In minor form he never indeed equalled Théophile Gautier, to whom he significantly dedicated his poems: in the best of the slight verse of Gautier there is a satisfaction, a balance of inwards and form, which we do not find in Baudelaire. He had a greater technical ability than Gautier, and yet the content of feeling is constantly bursting the receptacle. His apparatus, by which I do not mean his command of words and rhythms, but his stock of imagery (and every poet's stock of imagery is circumscribed somewhere), is not wholly perdurable or adequate. His prostitutes, mulattoes, Jewesses, ser-

pents, cats, corpses form a machinery which has not
worn very well; his Poet, or his Don Juan, has a romantic ancestry which is too clearly traceable. Compare with the costumery of Baudelaire the stock of
imagery of the *Vita Nuova*, or of Cavalcanti, and you
find Baudelaire's does not everywhere wear as well
as that of several centuries earlier; compare him
with Dante or Shakespeare, for what such a comparison is worth, and he is found not only a much
smaller poet, but one in whose work much more that
is perishable has entered.

To say this is only to say that Baudelaire belongs
to a definite place in time. Inevitably the offspring
of romanticism, and by his nature the first counter-
romantic in poetry, he could, like anyone else, only
work with the materials which were there. It must
not be forgotten that a poet in a romantic age cannot
be a "classical" poet except in tendency. If he is sincere, he must express with individual differences the
general state of mind—not as a *duty*, but simply because he cannot help participating in it. For such
poets, we may expect often to get much help from
reading their prose works and even notes and diaries;
help in deciphering the discrepancies between head
and heart, means and end, material and ideals.

What preserves Baudelaire's poetry from the fate
of most French poetry of the nineteenth century up
to his time, and has made him, as M. Valéry has said
in a recent introduction to the *Fleurs du Mal*, the one
modern French poet to be widely read abroad, is not
quite easy to conclude. It is partly that technical
mastery which can hardly be overpraised, and which

has made his verse an inexhaustible study for later poets, not only in his own language. When we read

> *Maint joyau dort enseveli*
> *Dans les ténèbres et l'oubli,*
> *Bien loin des pioches et des sondes;*
> *Mainte fleur épanche à regret*
> *Son parfum doux comme un secret*
> *Dans les solitudes profondes,*

we might for a moment think it a more lucid bit of Mallarmé; and so original is the arrangement of words that we might easily overlook its borrowing from Gray's *Elegy*. When we read

> *Valse mélancolique et langoureux vertige!*

we are already in the Paris of Laforgue. Baudelaire gave to French poets as generously as he borrowed from English and American poets. The renovation of the versification of Racine has been mentioned often enough; quite genuine, but might be over-emphasized, as it sometimes comes near to being a trick. But even without this, Baudelaire's variety and resourcefulness would still be immense.

Furthermore, besides the stock of images which he used that seems already second-hand, he gave new possibilities to poetry in a new stock of imagery of contemporary life.

> *. . . Au cœur d'un vieux faubourg, labyrinthe fangeux*
> *Où l'humanité grouille en ferments orageux,*
> *On voit un vieux chiffonnier qui vient, hochant la tête,*
> *Buttant, et se cognant aux murs comme un poète.*

This introduces something new, and something universal in modern life. (The last line quoted, which in ironic terseness anticipates Corbière, might be contrasted with the whole poem *Bénédiction* which begins the volume.) It is not merely in the use of imagery of common life, not merely in the use of imagery of the sordid life of a great metropolis, but in the elevation of such imagery to the *first intensity* —presenting it as it is, and yet making it represent something much more than itself—that Baudelaire has created a mode of release and expression for other men.

This invention of language, at a moment when French poetry in particular was famishing for such invention, is enough to make of Baudelaire a great poet, a great landmark in poetry. Baudelaire is indeed the greatest exemplar in *modern* poetry in any language, for his verse and language is the nearest thing to a complete renovation that we have experienced. But his renovation of an attitude towards life is no less radical and no less important. In his verse, he is now less a model to be imitated or a source to be drained than a reminder of the duty, the consecrated task, of sincerity. From a fundamental sincerity he could not deviate. The superficies of sincerity (as I think has not always been remarked) is not always there. As I have suggested, many of his poems are insufficiently removed from their romantic origins, from Byronic paternity and Satanic fraternity. The "satanism" of the Black Mass was very much in the air; in exhibiting it Baudelaire is the voice of his time; but I would observe that in Baudelaire, as in no one else, it is redeemed by *meaning something else*. He uses the same paraphernalia, but cannot limit its symbolism even to all that of which he is conscious. Compare him with Huysmans in *A Rebours, En Route,* and *Là-bas.* Huysmans, who is a first-rate realist of his time, only succeeds in making his diabolism interesting when he treats it externally, when he is merely describing a manifestation of his period (if such it was). His own interest in such matters is, like his interest in Christianity, a petty affair. Huysmans merely provides a document. Baudelaire would not even provide that, if he had been really absorbed in that ridiculous hocus-pocus. But actually Baudelaire is concerned, not with demons, black masses, and romantic blasphemy, but with the real problem of good and evil. It is hardly more than an accident of time that he uses the current imagery and vocabulary of blasphemy. In the middle nineteenth century, the age which (at its best) Goethe had prefigured, an age of bustle, programmes, platforms, scientific progress, humanitarianism and revolutions which improved nothing, an age of progressive degradation, Baudelaire perceived that what really matters is Sin and Redemption. It is a proof of his honesty that he went as far as he could honestly go and no further. To a mind observant of the post-Voltaire France (*Voltaire . . . le prédicateur des concierges*), a mind which saw the world of *Napoléon le petit* more lucidly than did that of Victor Hugo, a mind which at the same time had no affinity for the *Saint-Sulpicerie* of the day, the recognition of the reality of Sin is a New Life; and the possibility of damnation is so immense a relief in a world of electoral reform, plebiscites, sex reform and dress reform, that damnation itself is an immediate form of salvation—of salvation from the ennui of modern life, because it at last gives some significance to living. It is this, I believe, that Baudelaire is trying to express; and it is this which separates him from the modernist Protestantism of Byron and Shelley. It is apparently Sin in the Swinburnian sense, but really Sin in the permanent Christian sense, that occupies the mind of Baudelaire.

Yet, as I said, the sense of Evil implies the sense of good. Here too, as Baudelaire apparently confuses, and perhaps did confuse, Evil with its theatrical representations, Baudelaire is not always certain in his notion of the Good. The romantic idea of Love is never quite exorcized, but never quite surrendered to. In *Le Balcon*, which M. Valéry considers, and I think rightly, one of Baudelaire's most beautiful poems, there is all the romantic idea, but something more: the reaching out towards something which cannot be had *in*, but which may be had partly *through*, personal relations. Indeed, in much romantic poetry the sadness is due to the exploitation of the fact that no human relations are adequate to human desires, but also to the disbelief in any further object for human desires than that which, being human, fails to satisfy them. One of the unhappy necessities of human existence is that we have to "find things out for ourselves". If it were not so, the statement of Dante would, at least for poets, have done once for all. Baudelaire has all the romantic sorrow, but invents a new kind of romantic nostalgia—a derivative of his nostalgia being the *poésie des départs*, the *poésie des salles d'attente*. In a beautiful paragraph of the volume in question, *Mon Cœur Mis à Nu*, he imagines the vessels lying in harbour as saying: *Quand partons-nous vers le bonheur?* and his minor successor Laforgue exclaims: *Comme ils sont beaux, les trains manqués.* The poetry of flight—which, in contemporary France, owes a great debt to the poems of the A. O. Barnabooth of Valéry Larbaud—is, in its origin in this paragraph of Baudelaire, a dim recognition of the direction of beatitude.

But in the adjustment of the natural to the spiritual, of the bestial to the human and the human to the supernatural, Baudelaire is a bungler compared with Dante; the best that can be said, and that is a very great deal, is that what he knew he found out for himself. In his book, the *Journaux Intimes*, and especially in *Mon Cœur Mis à Nu*, he has a great deal to say of the love of man and woman. One aphorism which has been especially noticed is the following: *la volupté unique et suprême de l'amour gît dans la certitude de faire le mal.* This means, I think, that Baudelaire has perceived that what distinguishes the relations of man and woman from the copulation of beasts is the knowledge of Good and Evil (of *moral* Good and Evil which are not natural Good and Bad or Puritan Right and Wrong). Having an imperfect, vague romantic conception of Good, he was at least able to understand that the sexual act as evil is more dignified, less boring, than as the natural, "life-giving", cheery automatism of the modern world.

For Baudelaire, sexual operation is at least something not analogous to Kruschen Salts.

So far as we are human, what we do must be either evil or good; so far as we do evil or good, we are human; and it is better, in a paradoxical way, to do evil than to do nothing: at least, we exist. It is true to say that the glory of man is his capacity for salvation; it is also true to say that his glory is his capacity for damnation. The worst that can be said of most of our malefactors, from statesmen to thieves is that they are not men enough to be damned. Baudelaire was man enough for damnation: whether he *is* damned is, of course, another question, and we are not prevented from praying for his repose. In all his humiliating traffic with other beings, he walked secure in this high vocation, that he was capable of a damnation denied to the politicians and the newspaper editors of Paris.

[From *Baudelaire*. 1930.]

Part 4

RELIGION AND SOCIETY

CHRISTIANITY AND SOCIETY

~~~~~~

The Idea of a Christian Society is one which we can accept or reject; but if we are to accept it, we must treat Christianity with a great deal more *intellectual* respect than is our wont; we must treat it as being for the individual a matter primarily of thought and not of feeling. The consequences of such an attitude are too serious to be acceptable to everybody: for when the Christian faith is not only felt, but thought, it has practical results which may be inconvenient. For to see the Christian faith in this way—and to see it in this way is not necessarily to accept it, but only to understand the real issues—is to see that the difference between the Idea of a Neutral Society (which is that of the society in which we live at present) and the Idea of a Pagan Society (such as the upholders of democracy abominate) is, in the long run, of minor importance. I am not at this moment concerned with the means for bringing a Christian Society into existence; I am not even primarily concerned with making it appear desirable; but I am very much concerned with making clear its difference from the kind of society in which we are now living. Now, to understand the society in which he lives, must be to the interest of every conscious thinking person. The current terms in which we describe our society, the contrasts with other societies by which we—of the "Western Democracies"—eulogize it, only operate to deceive and stupefy us. To speak of ourselves as a Christian Society, in contrast to that of Germany or Russia, is an abuse of terms. We mean only that we have a society in which no one is penalized for the *formal profession* of Christianity; but we conceal from ourselves the unpleasant knowledge of the real values by which we live. We conceal from ourselves, moreover, the similarity of our society to those which we execrate: for we should have to admit, if we recognized the similarity, that the foreigners do better. I suspect that in our loathing of totalitarianism, there is infused a good deal of admiration for its efficiency.

[From *The Idea of a Christian Society*. 1939.]

"CHRISTIAN" OR "PAGAN"

We are living at present in a kind of doldrums between opposing winds of doctrine, in a period in which one political philosophy has lost its cogency for behaviour, though it is still the only one in which public speech can be framed. This is very bad for the English language; it is this disorder (for which we are all to blame) and not individual insincerity, which is responsible for the hollowness of many political and ecclesiastical utterances. You have only to examine the mass of newspaper leading articles, the mass of political exhortation, to appreciate the fact that good prose cannot be written by a people without convictions. The fundamental objection to fascist doctrine, the one which we conceal from ourselves because it might condemn ourselves as well, is that it is pagan. There are other objections too, in the political and economic sphere, but they are not objections that we can make with dignity until we set our own affairs in order. There are still other objections, to oppression and violence and cruelty, but however strongly we feel, these are objections to means and not to ends. It is true that we sometimes use the word "pagan", and in the same context refer to ourselves as "Christian". But we always dodge the real issue. Our newspapers have done all they could with the red herring of the "German national religion", an eccentricity which is after all no odder than some cults held in Anglo-Saxon countries: this "German national religion" is comforting in that it persuades us that *we* have a Christian civilization; it helps to disguise the fact that our aims, like Germany's, are materialistic. And the last thing we should like to do would be to examine the "Christianity" which, in such contexts as this, we say we keep.

[From *The Idea of a Christian Society*. 1939.]

WAR

In face of any naturally horrifying phenomenon like war we must measure the suffering, direct and indirect, against the spiritual goods which may come of suffering. We may find that the proportion of futile suffering, and of that kind of suffering which makes men worse rather than better, which abates their human dignity and deadens their sense of responsibility, is far too high; and that the total effect is at best one of futility. What we have to concern ourselves with primarily is the causes in modern society, in our industrial and financial machinery it may be, which bring about the *kind* of war which we have experienced; and to give our adherence to all alterations in that machinery which tend to remove the motives. We do not, I suppose, deny that society is very deeply affected morally and spiritually by material conditions, even by a machinery which it has constructed piecemeal and with short-sighted aims. This is not to accept any doctrine of determinism, for it means no more than that society, and the majority of individuals composing it, are only imperfectly conscious of what they are doing, directed by impure motives and aiming at false goods.

[From *Catholicism and the International Order*. 1934.]

"PRIVATE RELIGIONS"

I suspect that there is some taint of Original H. G. Wells about most of us in English-speaking countries; and that we enjoy drawing general conclusions from particular disciplines, using our accomplishment in one field as the justification for theorizing about the world in general. It is also a weakness of Anglo-Saxons to like to hold personal and private religions and to promulgate them. And when a scientist gets loose into the field of religion, all that he can do is to give us the impression which his scientific knowledge and thought has produced upon his everyday, and usually commonplace, personal and private imagination.

[From *Thoughts after Lambeth.* 1931.]

THE REFORMATION OF SOCIETY

No scheme for a change of society can be made to appear immediately palatable, except by falsehood, until society has become so desperate that it will accept any change. A Christian society only becomes acceptable after you have fairly examined the alternatives. We might, of course, merely sink into an apathetic decline: without faith, and therefore without faith in ourselves; without a philosophy of life, either Christian or pagan; and without art. Or we might get a "totalitarian democracy", different but having much in common with other pagan societies, because we shall have changed step by step in order to keep pace with them: a state of affairs in which we shall have regimentation and conformity, without respect for the needs of the individual soul; the puritanism of a hygienic morality in the interest of efficiency; uniformity of opinion through propaganda, and art only encouraged when it flatters the official doctrines of the time. To those who can imagine, and are therefore repelled by, such a prospect, one can assert that the only possibility of control and balance is a religious control and balance; that the only hopeful course for a society which would thrive and continue its creative activity in the arts of civilization, is to become Christian. That prospect involves, at least, discipline, inconvenience and discomfort: but here as hereafter the alternative to hell is purgatory.

[From *The Idea of a Christian Society*. 1939.]

THE STRAIT GATE

~~~~~~

There is no good in making Christianity easy and pleasant; "Youth", or the better part of it, is more likely to come to a difficult religion than to an easy one. For some, the intellectual way of approach must be emphasized; there is need of a more intellectual laity. For them and for others, the way of discipline and asceticism must be emphasized; for even the humblest Christian layman can and must live what, in the modern world, is comparatively an ascetic life. Discipline of the emotions is even rarer, and in the modern world still more difficult, than discipline of the mind; some eminent lay preachers of "discipline" are men who know only the latter. Thought, study, mortification, sacrifice: it is such notions as these that should be impressed upon the young— who differ from the young of other times merely in having a different middle-aged generation behind them. You will never attract the young by making Christianity easy; but a good many can be attracted by finding it difficult: difficult both to the disorderly mind and to the unruly passions.

[From *Thoughts after Lambeth*. 1931.]

A CHRISTIAN COMMUNITY

For the great mass of humanity whose attention is occupied mostly by their direct relation to the soil, or the sea, or the machine, and to a small number of persons, pleasures and duties, two conditions are required. The first is that, as their capacity for *thinking* about the objects of faith is small, their Christianity may be almost wholly realized in behaviour: both in their customary and periodic religious observances, and in a traditional code of behaviour towards their neighbours. The second is that, while they should have some perception of how far their lives fall short of Christian ideals, their religious and social life should form for them a natural whole, so that the difficulty of behaving as Christians should not impose an intolerable strain. These two conditions are really the same differently stated; they are far from being realized to-day.

The traditional unit of the Christian Community in England is the parish. I am not here concerned with the problem of how radically this system must be modified to suit a future state of things. The parish is certainly in decay, from several causes of which the least cogent is the division into sects: a much more important reason is urbanization—in which I am including also *sub*-urbanization, and all the causes and effects of urbanization. How far the parish must be superseded will depend largely upon our view of the necessity of accepting the causes which tend to destroy it. In any case, the parish will serve my purpose as an example of a community unit. For this unit must not be solely religious, and not solely social; nor should the individual be a member of two separate, or even overlapping units, one religious and the other social. The unitary community should be religious-social, and it must be one in which all classes, if you have classes, have their centre of interest. That is a state of affairs which is no longer wholly realized except in very primitive tribes indeed.

It is a matter of concern not only in this country, but has been mentioned with concern by the late Supreme Pontiff, speaking not of one country but of all civilized countries, that the masses of the people have become increasingly alienated from Christianity. In an industrialized society like that of England, I am surprised that the people retains as much Christianity as it does. For the great majority of the people—and I am not here thinking of social classes, but of intellectual strata—religion must be primarily a matter of behaviour and habit, must be integrated with its social life, with its business and its pleasures, and the specifically religious emotions must be a kind of extension and sanctification of the domestic and social emotions. Even for the most highly developed and conscious individual, living in the world, a consciously Christian direction of thought and feeling can only occur at particular moments during the day and during the week, and these moments themselves recur in consequence of formed habits; to be conscious, without remission, of a Christian and a non-Christian alternative at moments of choice, imposes a very great strain. The mass of the population, in a Christian society, should not be exposed to a way of life in which there is too sharp and frequent a conflict between what is easy for them or what their circumstances dictate and what is Christian. The compulsion to live in such a way that Christian behaviour is only possible in a restricted number of situations, is a very powerful force against Christianity; for behaviour is as potent to affect belief, as belief to affect behaviour.

I am not presenting any idyllic picture of the rural parish, either present or past, in taking as a norm, the idea of a small and mostly self-contained group attached to the soil and having its interests centred in a particular place, with a kind of unity which may be designed, but which also has to grow through generations. It is the idea, or ideal, of a community small enough to consist of a nexus of direct personal relationships, in which all iniquities and turpitudes will take the simple and easily appreciable form of wrong relations between one person and another. But at present not even the smallest community, unless so primitive as to present objectionable features of another kind, is so simplified as this; and I am not advocating any complete reversion to any earlier state of things, real or idealized. The example appears to offer no solution to the problem of industrial, urban and suburban life which is that of the majority of the population. In its religious organization, we may say that Christendom has remained fixed at the stage of development suitable to a simple agricultural and piscatorial society, and that modern material organization—or if "organization" sounds too complimentary, we will say "complication"— has produced a world for which Christian social forms are imperfectly adapted. Even if we agree on this point, there are two simplifications of the problem which are suspect. One is to insist that the only salvation for society is to return to a simpler mode of life, scrapping all the constructions of the modern world that we can bring ourselves to dispense with. This is an extreme statement of the neo-Ruskinian view, which was put forward with much vigour by the late A. J. Penty. When one considers the large amount of determination in social structure, this policy appears Utopian: if such a way of life ever comes to pass, it will be—as may well happen in the long run—from natural causes, and not from the moral will of men. The other alternative is to accept the modern world as it is and simply try to adapt Christian social ideals to it. The latter resolves itself into a mere doctrine of expediency; and is a surrender of the faith that Christianity itself can play any part in shaping social forms. And it does not require a Christian attitude to perceive that the modern system of society has a great deal in it that is inherently bad.

[From *The Idea of a Christian Society*. 1939.]

141

SOCIETY AND THE ARTS

What are the most fruitful social conditions for the production of works of the first order, philosophical, literary, or in the other arts, is perhaps one of those topics of controversy more suitable for conversation than for writing about. There may perhaps be no one set of conditions most suitable for the efflorescence of all these activities; it is equally possible that the necessary conditions may vary from one country and civilization to another. The régime of Louis XIV or of the Tudors and Stuarts could hardly be called libertarian; on the other hand, the rule of authoritarian governments in our time does not appear conducive to a renascence of the arts. Whether the arts flourish best in a period of growth and expansion, or in one of decay, is a question that I cannot answer. A strong and even tyrannous government may do no harm, so long as the sphere of its control is strictly limited; so long as it limits itself to restricting the liberties, without attempting to influence the minds, of its subjects; but a régime of unlimited demagogy appears to be stultifying. I must restrict my consideration to the position of the arts in our present society, and to what it should be in such a future society as I envisage.

It may be that the conditions unfavourable to the arts to-day lie too deep and are too extensive to depend upon the differences between one form of government and another; so that the prospect before us is either of slow continuous decay or of sudden extinction. You cannot, in any scheme for the reformation of society, aim directly at a condition in which the arts will flourish: these activities are probably by-products for which we cannot deliberately arrange the conditions. On the other hand, their decay may always be taken as a symptom of some social ailment to be investigated. The future of art and thought in a democratic society does not appear any brighter than any other, unless democracy is to mean something very different from anything actual. It is not that I would defend a moral censorship: I have always expressed strong objections to the suppression of books possessing, or even laying claim to literary merit. But what is more insidious than any censorship, is the steady influence which operates silently in any mass society organized for profit, for the depression of standards of art and culture. The increasing organization of advertisement and propaganda—or the influencing of masses of men by any means except through their intelligence—is all against them. The economic system is against them; the chaos of ideals and confusion of thought in our large scale mass education is against them; and against them also is the disappearance of any class of people who recognize public and private responsibility of patronage of the best that is made and written. At a period in which each nation has less and less "culture" for its own consumption, all are making furious efforts to export their culture, to impress upon each other their achievements in arts which they are ceasing to cultivate or understand. And just as those who should be the intellectuals regard theology as a special study, like numismatics or heraldry, with which they need not concern themselves, and theologians observe the same indifference to literature and art, as special studies which do not concern *them*, so our political classes regard both fields as territories of which they have no reason to be ashamed of remaining in complete ignorance. Accordingly the more serious authors have a limited, and even provincial audience, and the more popular write for an illiterate and uncritical mob.

[From *The Idea of a Christian Society*. 1939.]

RELIGION AND LITERATURE

~~~~~~

What I have to say is largely in support of the following propositions: Literary criticism should be completed by criticism from a definite ethical and theological standpoint. In so far as in any age there is common agreement on ethical and theological matters, so far can literary criticism be substantive. In ages like our own, in which there is no such common agreement, it is the more necessary for Christian readers to scrutinize their reading, especially of works of imagination, with explicit ethical and theological standards. The "greatness" of literature cannot be determined solely by literary standards; though we must remember that whether it is literature or not can be determined only by literary standards.

We have tacitly assumed, for some centuries past, that there is *no* relation between literature and theology. This is not to deny that literature—I mean, again, primarily works of imagination—has been, is, and probably always will be judged by some moral standards. But moral judgements of literary works are made only according to the moral code accepted by each generation, whether it lives according to that code or not. In an age which accepts some precise Christian theology, the common code may be fairly orthodox: though even in such periods the common code may exalt such concepts as "honour", "glory", or "revenge" to a position quite intolerable to Christianity. The dramatic ethics of the Elizabethan Age offers an interesting study. But when the common code is detached from its theological background, and is consequently more and more merely a matter of habit, it is exposed both to prejudice and to change. At such times morals are open to being altered *by* literature; so that we find in practice that what is "objectionable" in literature is merely what the present generation is not used to. It is a commonplace that what shocks one generation is accepted quite calmly by the next. This adaptability to change of moral standards is sometimes greeted with satisfaction as an evidence of human perfectibility: whereas it is only evidence of what unsubstantial foundations people's moral judgements have.

[From *Religion and Literature*. 1934.]

CHURCH AND STATE

To identify any particular form of government with Christianity is a dangerous error: for it confounds the permanent with the transitory, the absolute with the contingent. Forms of government, and of social organization, are in constant process of change, and their operation may be very different from the theory which they are supposed to exemplify. A theory of the State may be, explicitly or implicitly, anti-Christian: it may arrogate rights which only the Church is entitled to claim, or pretend to decide moral questions on which only the Church is qualified to pronounce. On the other hand, a régime may in practice claim either more or less than it professes, and we have to examine its workings as well as its constitution. We have no assurance that a democratic régime might not be as inimical to Christianity in practice, as another might be in theory: and the best government must be relative to the character and the stage of intelligence and education of a particular people in a particular place at a particular time. Those who consider that a discussion of the nature of a Christian society should conclude by supporting a particular form of political organization, should ask themselves whether they really believe our form of government to be more important than our Christianity; and those who are convinced that the present form of government of Britain is the one most suitable for any Christian people, should ask themselves whether they are confusing a Christian society with a society in which individual Christianity is tolerated.

Our preoccupation with foreign politics during the last few years has induced a surface complacency rather than a consistent attempt at self-examination of conscience. Sometimes we are almost persuaded that we are getting on very nicely, with a reform here and a reform there, and would have been getting on still better, if only foreign governments did not insist upon breaking all the rules and playing what is really a different game. What is more depressing still is the thought that only fear or jealousy of foreign success can alarm us about the health of our own nation; that only through this anxiety can we see such things as depopulation, mal-nutrition, moral deterioration, the decay of agriculture, as evils at all. And what is worst of all is to advocate Christianity, not because it is true, but because it might be beneficial. Towards the end of 1938 we experienced a wave of revivalism which should teach us that folly is not the prerogative of any one political party or any one religious communion, and that hysteria is not the privilege of the uneducated. The Christianity expressed has been vague, the religious fervour has been a fervour for democracy. It may engender nothing better than a disguised and peculiarly sanctimonious nationalism, accelerating our progress towards the paganism which we say we abhor. To justify Christianity because it provides a foundation of morality, instead of showing the necessity of Christian morality from the truth of Christianity, is a very dangerous inversion; and we may reflect, that a good deal of the attention of totalitarian states has been devoted, with a steadiness of purpose not always found in democracies, to providing their national life with a foundation of morality—the wrong kind perhaps, but a good deal more of it. It is not enthusiasm, but dogma, that differentiates a Christian from a pagan society.

It is very easy for speculation on a possible Christian order in the future to tend to come to rest in a kind of apocalyptic vision of a golden age of virtue. But we have to remember that the Kingdom of Christ on earth will never be realized, and also that it is always being realized; we must remember that whatever reform or revolution we carry out, the result will always be a sordid travesty of what human society should be—though the world is never left wholly without glory. In such a society as I imagine, as in any that is not petrified, there will be innumerable seeds of decay. Any human scheme for society is realized only when the great mass of humanity has become adapted to it; but this adaptation becomes also, insensibly, an adaptation of the scheme itself to the mass on which it operates: the overwhelming pressure of mediocrity, sluggish and indomitable as a glacier, will mitigate the most violent, and depress

149

the most exalted revolution, and what is realized is so unlike the end that enthusiasm conceived, that foresight would weaken the effort.

[From *The Idea of a Christian Society*. 1939.]

"CONFORMITY TO NATURE"

~~~~~

We may say that religion, as distinguished from modern paganism, implies a life in conformity with nature. It may be observed that the natural life and the supernatural life have a conformity to each other which neither has with the mechanistic life: but so far has our notion of what is natural become distorted, that people who consider it "unnatural"and therefore repugnant, that a person of either sex should elect a life of celibacy, consider it perfectly "natural" that families should be limited to one or two children. It would perhaps be more natural, as well as in better conformity with the Will of God, if there were more celibates and if those who were married had larger families. But I am thinking of "conformity to nature" in a wider sense than this. We are being made aware that the organization of society on the principle of private profit, as well as public destruction, is leading both to the deformation of humanity by unregulated industrialism, and to the exhaustion of natural resources, and that a good deal of our material progress is a progress for which succeeding generations may have to pay dearly. I need only mention, as an instance now very much before the public eye, the results of "soil-erosion"—the exploitation of the earth, on a vast scale for two generations, for commercial profit: immediate benefits leading to dearth and desert. I would not have it thought that I condemn a society because of its material ruin, for that would be to make its material success a sufficient test of its excellence; I mean only that a wrong attitude towards nature implies, somewhere, a wrong attitude towards God, and that the consequence is an inevitable doom. For a long enough time we have believed in nothing but the values arising in a mechanized, commercialized, urbanized way of life: it would be as well for us to face the permanent conditions upon which God allows us to live upon this planet. And without sentimentalizing the life of the savage, we might practise the humility to observe, in some of the societies upon which we look down as primitive or backward, the operation of a social-religious-artistic complex which we should emulate upon a higher plane. We have been accustomed to regard "progress" as always integral; and have yet to learn that it is only by an effort and a discipline, greater than society has yet seen the need of imposing upon itself, that material knowledge and power is gained without loss of spiritual knowledge and power. The struggle to recover the sense of relation to nature and to God, the recognition that even the most primitive feelings should be part of our heritage, seems to me to be the explanation and justification of the life of D. H. Lawrence, and the excuse for his aberrations. But we need not only to learn how to look at the world with the eyes of a Mexican Indian— and I hardly think that Lawrence succeeded—and we certainly cannot afford to stop there. We need to know how to see the world as the Christian Fathers saw it; and the purpose of reascending to origins is that we should be able to return, with greater spiritual knowledge, to our own situation. We need to recover the sense of religious fear, so that it may be overcome by religious hope.

[From *The Idea of a Christian Society*. 1939.]

MODERN EDUCATION

~~~~~~

Questions of education are frequently discussed as if they bore no relation to the social system in which and for which the education is carried on. This is one of the commonest reasons for the unsatisfactoriness of the answers. It is only within a particular social system that a system of education has any meaning. If education to-day seems to deteriorate, if it seems to become more and more chaotic and meaningless, it is primarily because we have no settled and satisfactory arrangement of society, and because we have both vague and diverse opinions about the kind of society we want. Education is a subject which cannot be discussed in a void: our questions raise other questions, social, economic, financial, political. And the bearings are on more ultimate problems even than these: to know what we want in education we must know what we want in general, we must derive our theory of education from our philosophy of life. The problem turns out to be a religious problem.

The progress (I do not mean the extension) of education for several centuries has been from one aspect a drift, from another aspect a push; for it has tended to be dominated by the idea of *getting on*. The individual wants more education, not as an aid to the acquisition of wisdom but in order to get on; the nation wants more in order to get the better of other nations, the class wants it to get the better of other classes, or at least to hold its own against them. Education is associated therefore with technical efficiency on the one hand, and with rising in society on the other. Education becomes something to which everybody has a "right", even irrespective of his capacity; and when everyone gets it—by that time, of course, in a diluted and adulterated form—then we naturally discover that education is no longer an infallible means of getting on, and people turn to another fallacy: that of "education for leisure"— without having revised their notions of "leisure". As soon as this precious motive of snobbery evaporates, the zest has gone out of education; if it is not going to mean more money, or more power over others, or a better social position, or at least a steady and respectable job, few people are going to take the trouble to acquire education. For deteriorate it as you may, education is still going to demand a good deal of drudgery. And the majority of people are incapable of enjoying leisure—that is, unemployment *plus* an income and a status of respectability—in any but pretty simple forms—such as balls propelled by hand, by foot, and by engines or tools of various types; in playing cards; or in watching dogs, horses, or other men engage in feats of speed or skill. The uneducated man with an empty mind if he be free from financial anxiety or narrow limitation, and can obtain access to golf-clubs, dance halls, etc., is, for all I can see, as well equipped to fill his leisure contentedly as is the educated man.

[From *Modern Education and the Classics*. 1933.]

THE DECAY OF THE MUSIC-HALL

~~~~~

The middle classes, in England as elsewhere, under democracy, are morally dependent upon the aristocracy, and the aristocracy are subordinate to the middle class, which is gradually absorbing and destroying them. The lower class still exists; but perhaps it will not exist for long. In the music-hall comedians they find the expression and dignity of their own lives; and this is not found in the most elaborate and expensive revue. In England, at any rate, the revue expresses almost nothing. With the decay of the music-hall, with the encroachment of the cheap and rapid-breeding cinema, the lower classes will tend to drop into the same state of protoplasm as the bourgeoisie. The working man who went to the music-hall and saw Marie Lloyd and joined in the chorus was himself performing part of the act; he was engaged in that collaboration of the audience with the artist which is necessary in all art and most obviously in dramatic art. He will now go to the cinema, where his mind is lulled by continuous senseless music and continuous action too rapid for the brain to act upon, and will receive, without giving, in that same listless apathy with which the middle and upper classes regard any entertainment of the nature of art. He will also have lost some of his interest in life. Perhaps this will be the only solution. In an interesting essay in the volume of *Essays on the Depopulation of Melanesia*, the psychologist W. H. R. Rivers adduced evidence which has led him to believe that the natives of that unfortunate archipelago are dying out principally for the reason that the "Civilization" forced upon them has deprived them of all interest in life. They are dying from pure boredom. When every theatre has been replaced by 100 cinemas, when every musical instrument has been replaced by 100 gramophones, when every horse has been replaced by 100 cheap motor-cars, when electrical ingenuity has made it possible for every child to hear its bedtime stories from a loud-speaker, when applied science has done everything possible with the materials on this earth to make life as interesting as possible, it will not be surprising if the population of the entire civilized world rapidly follows the fate of the Melanesians.

[From *Marie Lloyd*. 1923.]